DEMOCRACY
Evil or Blessing

By: **Mushtaq Ahmad**

DEMOCRACY

Evil or Blessing

By: **<u>Mushtaq Ahmad</u>**

ARPress
ILLUMINATING IDEAS
EMPOWERING VOICES

ARPress
45 Dan Road Suite 5
Canton MA 02021
Hotline: 1(888) 821-0229
Fax: 1(508) 545-7580

Ordering Information:
Quantity sales. Special discounts are available on quantity purchases by corporations, associations, and others. For details, contact the publisher at the address above.

Printed in the United States of America.

ISBN-13:   Softcover   979-8-89330-941-6
            eBook   979-8-89330-940-9
Library of Congress Control Number: 2024902572

TO MY PARENTS

An effort has been made to bring out the good and bad points of present-day democracies in the light of recent world events. The readers can analyze and judge their elected and to be elected representatives as to their conduct for a better future democratic governance.

The misrepresentation of population consisting of voting and non-voting members in democratic governance has been highlighted. The nonvoting members are not allowed to participate in their democratic process until reaching the voting age, whereas, the voting members which do not participate willingly think that their presence will not bring any change towards better governance.

The writings are supported by the famous quotations of the wise and learned personalities of the world and newspaper reports.

The misrepresentations of the voters who voted by the elected members kicks in when these legislators move away from the election agenda by following the party leader going against the election agenda, as well as, start accommodating indirect parties.

The democratic process through very costly for the countries practicing democracies however does adopt to the changing requirements of the population.

ACKNOWLEDGEMENTS:

The writing of the book was not possible without the hard work, support, and patience of my wife Naveeda and my brother Mukhtar Ahmad.

LIST OF NARRATED RECENT EVENTS/NEWSPAPER CLIPPINGS

CHAPTER ONE

INTRODUCTION

INTRODUCTION

There is a saying that "A ruler can have no power without soldiers, no soldiers without money, no money without the well-being of his subjects, and no popular well-being without justice." Thus, justice in the society on all fronts weather it is social or economic is the basic condition for a just and right direction.

Kenneth Janda has done an excellent study to highlight the various variables and their interaction in a cross national survey of political parties in countries practicing democratic form of governments. Kenneth Janda has identified cultural differentiators like economic status, religion, ethnicity, region, urbanization, and education. Social cleavage of any sort is a common factor of social attraction, social concentration, and social reflection. Issues of religious, political, economic, class, national, language, justice, and corruption are highlighted in the study. Political parties' goal/orientation, strategy, and tactics employed to achieve the stated goals/objectives by various mixes of open competition, restricting party competition; using direct and indirect tactics for electoral competition are discussed in the study. Then there is AUTONOMY; "The degree to which organizations function free from others and thus generally occupy an independent place in society." And AUTONOMY; "as a party's structural independence from other institutions and organizations, whether in or out of country," AUTONOMY in a democratic form of government is nothing more than a dream that never comes true. Kenneth Janda has also included in the study available resources of funds, sources of members, sources of leaders, relations with domestic parties and foreign organizations. The political parties and their degree of organization, centralization of power, coherence, and involvement are also included in the study.

On the other hand, Peter Mair has segregated party organizations into three different elements/faces interacting with each other. Firstly, it is the "party in public office, that is, the party organization in government and in parliament". Secondly, it is "party on the ground, that is, the membership organization and also potentially the loyal party voters". Thirdly, it is the "party in central office which is organizationally distinct from the party in public office ---- usually representative of the party on the ground.

In the above two major studies political parties are at the centre of studies as present day democracies are run by political parties and their leadership. However, a different approach is taken in this book which examines the political party candidates at one end and the voting and non-voting population on the other end.

Effort has been made in the light of concatenated current events taking place the world over, to bring out both the good points and the bad points of present day democracies for the discerning reader to comprehend and judge for himself/herself their present governments/ legislators as to their conduct and status effecting the voter (who voted) and the voter (who did not vote), as well as, the general public who do not fall in the voters category because they are below 18 or 21 years of age and are thus not eligible to exercise their right to vote according to the constitution of different countries that they live in.

The book has been kept concise as the hectic present day engagements do not let the readers afford much time to face a lengthy folk lore, as against, to the point discussion, made easy to understand with the help of current events and quotations.

"The wisdom of the vice and the experience of the ages are perpetuated by quotations" BENJAMIN DISRAELI. (Page No.197-3500).

The world in adopting democracies has relinquished theocracy and moved away from religions, thus the parson has removed surplice, which cannot be thus identified and referred to. As against, the written/ evolved constitutions of the different countries; looked after like a sacred cow carved out of stone. Which can later on be re-carved or patched up according to the will of the legislators; not delivering the due benefit to the populous thus making them slaves of the democratic system which is a misnomer of plutocratic system of governance.

People in general, the world over have placed their religions behind the veil of material gains and the same reflects in present day democratic governance systems where majority of the people have forgotten the importance of religion in their lives. The state do not teach or develop in any country of the world, the code of conduct, from infancy to adulthood that is 18 years of age in some countries to 21 years of age in others. That is close to one third of a person's life is totally devoid of participation in the democratic system of governance, whereas, his/her income is taxable.

The constitutions of the countries and laws made by the legislatures do not teach the code of conduct to the people. It is never told publicly to the people that if you kill someone or you hurt someone or you steal something or you do a forbidden thing; that you will go to jail, unless you kill someone, or steal something, or do something that is forbidden that the law turns up on your door to tell you that you have to go to jail, for what you have done was a crime as stated in the law of the land.

The above commentary, however, thought to be unnecessary is necessary to make a point that the religion in the lives of the people from infancy to death is the foundation of code of conduct which has been bestowed on people by God through His Prophets, and holy books given to these Prophets throughout the ages.

Thus the absence of religion as a part of democratic governance, be it Judaism, Christianity, or Islam results in derogatory laws being made against the benefit to mankind like same sex marriages, abortion, etc prohibited by God. Thus the absence of religion from the democratic system of governance breeds fanaticism in every religion where the religious fanatics; against the very essence of their religious teachings; enforce their religious values on people by force and take part in subversive activities to support their religion, in fact, they are working against their religion which forbids the use of force in the practice of religion.

The profit motive of capitalism complementing democratic system of governance has resulted in flight of capital to countries with lower cost of production, resulting in excessive capacity for banking and service sectors due to constantly eroding industrial base. Thus leading to ever excessive budgetary deficits, financed by external resources in anticipation of an economic upswing which is not swinging into motion and choking the capitalist system through constantly/increasingly high unemployment in the wake of lacking structural adjustments.

"The ship of democracy, which has weathered all storms, may sink through the mutiny of those abroad." GROVER CLEVELAND. (Page No.70-3500)

CHAPTER TWO

REPRESENTATIVE DEMOCRACY

DEMOCRACY

We start by examining various definitions of democracy given in dictionaries – 'A form of Government in which the supreme power is vested in the people collectively and is administered by them or by officers appointed by them: the people specially the common people. "(Chamber's 20th Century Dictionary)," Democracy is Government by the people – a form of Government in which the supreme power is vested in people," (Oxford Dictionary), "Democracy is a political system in which people choose their Government by voting for them in election. " (Collins)

In the above three definitions one thing is common and that is the people and the one that closely matches the modern day majority of democracies in the world is given by Collins.

Democracy is a political system which runs according to the constitution of a country passed by the elected representatives which might be written or based upon traditions. The political system in practice involves a voter; a candidate who either represents a political party or is an independent within a constituency; time period generally runs four to five years after which elections are to be held, or else upon the fall of government or vacation of constituency seat by resignation/death, etc. of the elected candidate.

1. POLITICS: The art or science of government – the management of a political party, political affairs or opinions (US), maneuvering and intriguing (Chamber's) – The art or science of government – the management of a political party (Webster's) – Affairs of state, civics, government, government policy (Collins).

2. POLITICAL PARTIES: The political parties are formed; on the basis of common interests, common objectives, and common goals which once formed struggle for that cause to achieve the common objectives and goals which may be social, economic or religious, and to take part in an election of the country/practicing democratic system of government, with the aim to form a government and thus achieve the party members/voters objectives and goals.

Historically the political interests have been centered around-Left v/s Right, Conservative v/s Liberal, Black v/s White and so on. Every country in the world has different historical background leading to its formation and the formation of political parties in that historical context.

The political parties and their system of operation/management is a challenging task; whether it be voters loyalty/ignorance/interest/ acceptance of party agenda; rejection of party agenda or the worst comes to worst the disgruntled voters not voting at all for any candidate in the light of dismal performance of political parties in the past due to either not delivering the promised agenda or the absence of a suitable candidate to be voted in; whether it be party's management moves to remain in office by forming coalition/policy making and campaigning; whether it be managing the family owned political party in case of death/retirement of their leader as husband or wife, son or daughter, brother/sister to another brother/sister and so on taking over the party leadership.

3. CANDIDATE: A candidate is one who stands in an election from the constituency that he/she will represent the voters in the legislature – if elected. The candidate is normally a political party candidate; however, he could be an independent pursuing his individual policies and representing the constituency voters only instead of representing the political party and their members/voters.

4. CONSTITUENCY: This is the geographical distribution of a country, province/state, or district for electoral purposes. The elected representative from a constituency is sent to the legislature for which he/she contested election and got elected. There are various terms used for constituency like District (USA), Riding (Canada), Circonscription (France), Electorate (Australia and New Zealand), and Division (UK). Every member of a legislature represents his/her constituency voters who voted him/her in, in the election.

5. VOTER: A voter is one who is eligible to vote in an election (as defined by the constitution of the country) constituency where his/ her vote is exercised/counted/registered and in that election/poll he/ she expresses his/her opinion in an authorized formal way normally

through a ballot paper in which he/she ticks or stamps on the candidate of his choice.

6. VOTE: "An earnest desire: an expression of wish or opinion in an authorized formal way." (Chambers 20th Century)" A vote is a choice made by a particular person or group in a meeting or election." (Collins) "Formal expression of a wish or opinion – decision of a majority – express a choice by vote" (Webster's). "Act or power of expressing opinion or choice: a suffrage (voters right to vote)" (Webster's).

7. ELECTIONS: An election is the process of choosing a representative by the eligible voters for a certain period of time while exercising their right to vote as provided in the constitution/rules and regulations of the body holding elections. The elections could be for a trade union representatives, chamber of commerce and industry representatives, municipal body representatives, provincial body representatives and or federal body representatives. We will keep ourselves focused on elections for democratic system of governance where the political parties play a pivotal role.

The eligible voters from the general public of a country running a democratic system of governance are given the right to cast their votes for the available contesting candidates generally representing political parties in their constituency during the designated voting period in an election.

"The oppressed are allowed once every few years to decide which particular representative of the oppressing class are to represent and repress them "KARLMARX. (Page No.267-3500)

The voter votes for his choice of agenda, by voting for the available candidate of a political party that carries or closely matches his/her agenda for the next term of election.

"We would like to vote for the best man, but he is never a candidate" KIN HUBBARD

8. FREEDOM AND CHOICE: The democratic system of government provides restricted freedom (within the legal framework as to safeguard the rights of fellow citizens) of movement, speech,

assembly, choice of religion, choice of association, choice of vocation, equality of citizens and the right to acquire property.

Laws are written and passed by the elected representatives (after debating) as desired by the political party leaders in the context of party's election agenda be it at federal, provincial/state, municipal/city level.

9. SUPREMACY: Political party is supreme and the persons forming the party fall second.

The representative getting the most votes cast in his/her favor in the respective constituency in an election gets elected provided the elections were free, fair and transparent or else the misrepresentation kicks in by bogus votes, ghost polling stations, etc., etc., against the very essence of democracy.

"You do not have to fool all the people all of the time; you just have to fool enough to get elected" GERALD BARZAN. (Page No.184-3500)

The elected representatives of a credible election generally do listen to their constituents for solving their problems, as well as, keep a close liaison with their constituents as the same votes are again required for the next election to keep the candidate in avowed representation.

10. ONE WAY STREET: Democracy is a one way street for the voters of a country/ constituency where you can vote the candidates in the avowed representation in an election but you cannot vote them out; when you want to; if the party (candidates) you voted for fail's to deliver at one or more fronts; or because the party mortgaged the nation and national assets against their (the nation's) wishes. Thousands and thousands of people have been killed all around the world and are being killed daily during protests, strikes, demonstrations, to dislodge the democratic dictators all over the world mostly supported by powerful nations of the world for their own national and personal interests against the true essence of democratic, moral, and ethical values cherished by these powerful nations.

Above all, the political party in the government starts representing the indirect parties (like the influential powers World Bank, IMF and so on) in the legislature instead of representing the cause of their respective constituency voters, who voted them in.

Vote "**The instrument and symbol of a freeman's power to make a fool of himself and a wreck of his country.**" AMBROSE BIERCE (Page No.262-3500)

Democratic system of governance is functioning in most of the countries of the world, in some countries it is functioning under constitutional monarchies, while in the others, under the umbrella of political parties; most of the capitalist countries have bi-party and multi-party democracies, whereas, the communist countries have totalitarian, single party systems.

The constitutional monarchies of Europe have the least interference in democratic style of government, whereas, the governing Middle East monarchies have the most interference in the democratic style of their governments, as the total affairs of the governments are run by monarchies.

11. CAPITALISM AND DEMOCRACY: Democratic systems of governance go hand in hand with capitalism. Capitalism designates an economic system founded on capital and the economic activity is acquisition in terms of money.

In business "**He who has reaped the profits has committed the crime.**" SENECA. (Page No.46-3500)

The economic activity should take place in a competitive environment which is closely associated with personal risk where he/she is free to strive for economic gains in any way he/she chooses without violating the penal code in a rational economic spirit.

"**Unconscionableness, to define it, is a neglect of reputation for the pursuit of filthy lucre.** "THEOPHRASTUS. (Page No.45-3500)

"**Capitalism is something none of us know how to define it, but we called it generally the capitalist system – a complex of traditional usage, uncontrolled acquisitive energy and perverted opportunities wasting life.** "H.G. Wells. (Page No.46-3500)

12. **FREE- ENTERPRISE:** Capitalism is characterized by the absence of planning and presence of individual actions in private economies where market prices are a result of market forces and not government planning.

"**Let the buyer beware**." LATIN MAYIM. (Page No.46-3500)

Consumer is sovereign in a capitalist economy. People are free to choose their occupation for money and self realization. Enterprise is free to have private ownership or material means of production. The individuals are free to save, invest, inherit, and accumulate wealth. Competition is encouraged and monopoly is discouraged by the market forces.

EUROPE'S DEMOCRACY AT STAKE

The Dawn/Guardian News Services article by Amortya Sen titled "Europe's democracy at stake" printed in the Daily dawn Newspaper of Friday June 24, 2011 states that, "Europe has led the world in the practice of democracy. It is, therefore, worrying that the dangers to democratic governance today, coming through the back door of financial priority, are not receiving the attention they should." Two distinct issues have been identified in this article under the influence of financial agencies (due to some of the European Countries heavy borrowing from these agencies) and rating agencies (which drop the ratings of these countries after every additional borrowing due to the risk associated with non-payment of interest and principal in the light of stagnant/declining economic activity, resulting in, higher interest costs for these countries). The first issue concerns the country's democratic priorities where the financial institutions and rating agencies start commanding the democratically elected government to make the structural or other changes in various organs of the government in total disregard of the party policy/agenda based upon voter's choice and the second issue concerns the viability of financial stability after making these changes. Thus, the united democratic Europe under Euro currently confiscates the freedom of individual countries as regards to monetary policy and exchange rate adjustments which provide a huge help in these sort of crisis.

INDIA STUMBLES ON A LONG CORRUPTION

TRAIL: By JOHN ELLIOTT. A truck driver was reported to have been beaten to death by officials in North India earlier this week for not paying Rs.500/- bribe....

A former cabinet minister for telecoms, Dayanidhi Maran, is about to be charged for corruption in an ongoing telecoms scandal. He is the second ex-telecom minister to be charged in the case – the first, Andimuthu Raja, has been held in a Delhi jail since February pending trial, along with various others....

A crisis has split and preoccupied the top levels of the government in the past week over whether Pranab Mukherjee, the finance minister, tried some months ago in a ministry memo to implicate Palaniappan Chidambaram, his predecessor and now home minister, in that scandal. This has been partially and unsatisfactorily resolved tonight by a joint statement from the two men denying any rift...

A close adviser to former prime minister Atul Bihari Vajpayee was arrested earlier this week and is being held in jail for allegedly organizing bribes for votes when India's US nuclear deal was before parliament in 2008, as was a provincial Uttar Pradesh politician earlier this month...

This modern India – a proud but often dysfunctional country that aspires to be a world super power – just a month or so after it was caught up in an anti-corruption frenzy led Anna Hazare, a social campaigner. A Mahatma Gandhi look alike, Hazare marched, demonstrated, fasted, and humiliated the government with demands that a new corruption ombudsman, the Lok Pal, should have vide-ranging powers.

His campaign drew massive support from India's middle classes, especially but not exclusively the young, who were protesting not just against corruption but at the way the country is run by self-serving national politicians down to police and other brutal officials on the streets and in rural areas. **Chidambaram and Mukher-jee.**

The current scandal, which involves telecom licenses and spectrum that were issued by Raja to selected companies in 2008 at 2001 prices, was widely known about and criticized by the end of that year – see my blog article in November 2008. But no one in the government seriously tried to stop it.

In the past week, it seemed to threaten Chidambaram's ministerial job because of suggestions in Mukherjee's Finance Ministry memo that, when he was finance minister in 2008, Chidambaram abetted what was being done by Raja.

Chidambaram and MUKHER-JEE reportedly have differences that partly date from others scandals in financial services, and both looked grim when they appeared on the steps of the Finance Ministry this evening to make their joint statement. Tensions include reported bugging of **Mukher-jee's** office, which some people assumed was organized by Chidambaram's Home Ministry.

Prime Minister Manmohan Singh and his Congress Party political boss, Sonia Gandhi, have been working on the crisis which has threatened to spread beyond Chidambaram because so many parts of the government, including the prime minister's office, and Manmohan Singh himself, knew what Raja was doing and did not stop him.

The point here is that many cabinet ministers have direct links to leading companies, including some involved in the scandal such as Reliance Communications run by Anil Ambani, and the Essar Group run by the Ruia family. On the sidelines is Mukesh Ambani, who runs the separate Reliance Industries group. An active rival of his younger brother, he is also directly linked to ministers involved. Anil Ambani, it emerged today, is to be questioned by the Central Bureau of Investigation.

On top of all this, Subramanian Swamy, a campaigning lawyer and politician who triggered the Chidambaram and Mukher-jee crisis, said last night that he will produce evidence implicating Robert Vadra, Sonia Gandhi's son-in-law, whose business deals have received some publicity.

All this illustrates how corruption in India is now so widespread and deeply embedded that it can threaten the stability of the government. There seems little hope of stemming it – from officials' street-level bribes and killings to national scandals – despite the Hazare movement. **Token arrests.**

Certainly nothing significant has changed yet. A total of 14 politicians, bureaucrats and company executives have been arrested and jailed in Delhi pending trial on the telecom scandal, as have others on allegations over last year's Common Wealth Games (CWG) contracts and vote buying mentioned above. Elsewhere, politicians and businessmen involved in mining scandals have been arrested and jailed.

This is not however a genuine effort to demonstrate with arrests that corruption must stop. No significant politician or prominent businessman, nor anyone the government wants to protect, has yet been jailed. Those arrested include people who the government is prepared to sacrifice (at least temporarily) such as Suresh Kalmadi, who presided over the CWG, and his henchmen, plus Raja who belongs to the Tamil Nadu's DMK party and is dispensable, some political opponents, and three of Anil Ambani's senior executives.

On a broader front, the government has removed MP's patronage powers to issue land, telephone lines and petrol station licenses to favored friends and supporters – but that is only tinkering at the lowest and least important end of corruption. It has also been announced that prosecution of corrupt bureaucrats will be speeded up with stiffer penalties.

What has also happened, according to widespread anecdotal reports, is that officials at all levels of government are becoming so scared of facing corruption accusations that they are reluctant to take decisions. That is seriously delaying policy implementation in a government that already has a reputation internationally for muddled economic and industrial policies that discourage investors.

No-one in the government has emerged with the leadership ability or stature to tackle this malaise, and turn the Hazare movement into a positive campaign for curbing corruption. Manmohan Singh has neither the authority nor ability to lead. Sonia Gandhi, who has recently returned from the US after a suspected cancer operation, is not a potential public leader. Her son and heir, Rahul, has failed in recent weeks, notably while his mother was in the US, to do more than play a bit part.

That leaves the government perpetually on the back foot doing damage control, and there is no sign of that changing any time soon.

Indeed, it might worsen as more linkages with the telecom and other scandals emerge. – *Courtesy the Nation October 2, 2011.*

CHAPTER THREE

CONDUCT AND DEMOCRACY

CANDIDATE

The candidate could be an independent or a representative of a political party. The candidate has to have means to contest the election. An average citizen do not have the means to contest the election since it involves manning and maintaining an election office, spending on print, TV and Radio advertising and so on. In majority cases, the winning candidate remains in this illicit profession of politics, where, vocation turns to avocation for a life time.

Once you enter an election race as a candidate you are a gambler because your chance of losing or winning depends on the probability of your success in the race. You end up as a winner or loser after the election results are announced, however, when your objective is to gain popularity and be very well known to the public after spending all that money on lost election, you are always a winner. **"Politics is the diversion of trivial men who, where they succeed at it, became important in the eyes of more trivial men."** (George Jean Nathan). **(Page No.183-3500)**

On the other hand, the money you spent on election for getting elected to represent the voters who voted for you could very well be spent for the benefit of the people in your area on a benevolent project (like hospital, orphanage, education institutions, research facility, etc.) to help the poor and needy as against gaining an influential position for yourself..

O" An honest politicians is one who when lie's bought stays bought." (SIMON CAMERON). **(Page No.182-3500)**

The corruption starts taking effect when the person decides to stand as a candidate in an election race, as funds are needed to meet the election expenses. Once you are declared a winner your prime objective is to recover the money spent on your election campaign or else if the money has been put up by someone else then to start propagating his/her agenda/project, in order to return the favor, by providing that entity undue gains through misuse of public funds fully camouflaged under the umbrella of fair practices. The candidate upon his/her success and during service to the public and his/her representation of constituency voters in the legislature consciously does every- thing to recover his/her election expenses by affording undue gains to his/her fund providers, as well as, their own business empires, whereas, unconsciously he/she votes for the party platform that he/she stands on, or got elected. Thus the candidate as an elected representative starts favoring a few at the expense of the majority and sheltering few bad apples at the vast expense to the society, which results in denying the due and fair benefits expected of him/her by the common citizens like cheap daily usage products, good and efficient government services, low taxation and so on. The representative thus starts violating the fundamental rights of public at large that he/she is supposed to serve as dictated in their oath of office. The representative's character thus turns from bad to worse and this fact is very well known to him / her and his / her associates / financiers / helpers / relatives deriving undue benefits of him / her.

Hebrew Proverb "a rich man has no need of character." (Page No.49-3500)

"The universe seems bankrupt as soon as we begin to discuss the character of individuals" HENRY DAVID THORSON. (Page No.49-3500)

"Under-Neath this flabby exterior is an enormous lack of character" OSCAR LEVANT." (Page No.49-3500)

OATH OF OFFICE:

An oath of office from an appointed / elected / selected / inherited / default appointment and so on is a requirement which must be met before that person is recognized to be signatory of that office. The oath establishes a trust relationship between the oath taker and the subjects whose rights/interests he/she watches/defends in the ever presence of All Mighty in the case of the people of the book or else a conscious individual to keep his/her trust according to the norms of his/her religion/theology, etc.

The oath of office is administered by a figure recognized in the constitution/ tradition as 'under oath' and normally one step above the oath taker in public or private position. There are different practices in different countries of oath administration mostly by swearing while putting their hands up/or holding their respective holly books in their right hand. The practice of administrating oath of office by laying hands on the holy book or holding the book is naturally more authentic than taking an oath of office without the Holy Book; as it gives more strength to the person having good conduct to do justice with all the subjects, whereas, the oath without the Holy Book is frivolous and provides opportunities to person having bad conduct to avoid and escape the wrath of Almighty as they have not laid hands on or held the Holy Book in their hands, thus avoiding physical contact also makes the oath of office frivolous and thereafter committing breaches of trust at will with due consciousness that verbal oath without the book is not binding on him/her as it would be with the Holy Book in his/her hand.

"I will take thy word for faith, not as thine oath; who shuns not to break one will sure crack both, "(William Shakespeare). (Page No.167-3500)

The oaths of office for public servants and political appointees in general owe allegiance to protect and preserve the constitution whether written or evolved traditionally and owe allegiance to the country, as well as, to do justice between and to all. The violation of oath is taken for granted in countries full of corruption/worst conduct/and distanced from the true religious values. In some cases the oath takers do not meet the conditions of eligibility as given in the constitution and as expounded in their respective religious books that they take oath on.

"When a man assumes a public trust he should consider himself a public property." (THOMAS JEFFERSON). (Page No.183-3500)

"Politics: A strife of interests masquerading as a contest of principles. The conduct of public affairs for private advantage." (AMBROSE BIERCE). (Page No.184-3500)

POLITICAL PARTIES

The political party that comes to power start's accommodating their financial donors / supporters / persons / groups / companies / industries, etc. through the use of public funds by putting forward and awarding projects of their choice and letting these people make these projects look beneficial in the eyes of awarders and the public, whereas, the case may be otherwise when explored and analyzed; like advertising contracts, public project contracts, special defense contracts, special infrastructure contracts, road repair and building contracts, special science project contracts, special space project contracts, etc. and the list goes on and on.

FEAR FACTOR

The above described favorite companies/industries often use 'FEAR FACTOR' to extort public money for private use, in the name of economy and jobs, i.e., the collapse of economic system and the fear of anarchy associated with this collapse. The 'FEAR' for the party in power to be dislodged by the public strikes, political agitation, mass protests against their policies, is one of the major factor used by this major group to extort money from the public till, for the benefit of the few who have created this opportunity for themselves to gain from the public funds, at almost nil cost to them, however, when the same money is lent out by them to the public at the going rate translates to profit extorted from the public for using their resources. The majority of billionaires/millionaires in the world are made through the use of public funds in the poor as well as rich countries alike.

The public is hit with double impact in case of deficit financing (for the aids and grants to the companies) by paying interest on the borrowed money and meeting the deficit through higher taxes, whereas, in the case of surplus budget the public pays for them by foregoing interest on these funds, as well as, losing the benefit of these funds being employed in public's welfare projects. The third impact is associated with paying the salaries of public servants who are managing these funds on behalf of the government.

"You must not enthrone ignorance just because there is so much of it." (AMERICAN PROVERB) (Page No.184-3500)

What a pity! The executive and officers of these big banks and auto companies, besides many others, in Europe and America are rewarded with big bonuses/salary packages for their failures.

"You can fool too many people too much of the time." (JAMES THURBER) (Page No.184-3500)

The 'FEAR FACTOR' is used to save the business (paper) empires on the pretext; of job losses (unemployment) that is so many people losing so many jobs; stimulating the economy; jump starting the economy by providing public funds to their political party associates, their own mafia groups whether it be in the case of direct funds to keep afloat the sinking ships or indirect funds by awarding projects and so on for their financial contributors.

SUBSIDIES:

Subsidies are provided for various industries and mostly to agriculture sector of the American and European Union Countries for keeping these industries healthy and alive at the cost to the public in the shape of higher taxes. The general public of these countries can only get the benefits of these subsidies if the products are made cheaper for them instead of paying higher taxes and higher prices for the products of these industries which get subsidies in return for their financial contribution to political parties; and the agricultural sector provides votes against the favor of subsidies, to the political parties.

"A straw vote only shows which way the hot air is blowing" HENRY. (Page No.262-3500)

NATIONAL PARASITES:

There are national parasites supported by the political parties in power for votes or getting support from the opposition parties, and or coalition parties like public airlines, railways, national interest industries, defense firms/industries, space firms/industry, steel industry, auto industry, public transit, banks, insurance, health, utilities and so on which thrive on tax money in the wake of their dismal performance/ higher than normal wages/highly inefficient management/resource wastefulness/; working under a unionized umbrella; threatening and sometimes meeting their threat of bringing the nation to a standstill by strikes. The staffs working in these so called public organizations are the stringiest parasites of the nations for utilizing public funds in the name of government support year after year. Every financial injection in the loss making public organization generally makes these parasites go from bad to worse except for a few face lifting's.

"If there is anything a public servant hates to do its something for the public." (KIN HUBBARD). (Page No.182-3500)

Thus the use of 'FEAR FACTOR' for causing massive unemployment, severe inconvenience to the nation, fear of dipping into recession and loss of popularity etc notions are used to channel massive public funds for the support of inefficient and irresponsible public organizations who are skillful absorbers of public funds without any credible accountability.

"For a little stealing dye gist you in jail soon or late. For the big stealing dye makes you emperor and puts you in the Hall of Fame when you croaks" (Page No.46-3500)

"A little stealing is a dangerous part. But stealing largely is a noble art; It means to rob a hen-roost of hen,

But stealing millions makes us gentlemen." EUGENE O'NEILL. (Page No.46-3500)

SPECIAL INTEREST GROUPS:

These are the most powerful groups ruling the most powerful nations in an autocratic dictatorial style under the fully camouflaged umbrella portraying (in the big bold letter) DEMOCRACY, the fruit of which the general public of these advanced countries have never enjoyed. The general public in these countries according to their norms is morally very good whereas the special interest groups are morally as bad to bring themselves, and have even brought themselves to the point of hatred by the general public.

"The right man, in the right place, at the right time – can steal millions." (GREGORY NUNN).184-3500

Special interest groups are formulated on different basis according to the common interests and benefits they share among each other, and with the elected representatives of the government that they are associated with. The basis of their formulation could be economic, social, psychological, special causes, religious, protectionism, and so on to mention a few. These special groups muster a forceful and incredible influence over legislature members, ministers and chief executives of their respective countries.

The special interest groups are staunch supporters of political parties in the shape of lobbyists, writers, speakers, retired politicians, bureaucrats, corporate heads, Heads of NGO's and so on; who support the political parties for winning the election; form a very strong mafia group to extort and channel the public funds towards their own ends. These strong mafia groups found almost in every democratic country, as well as, in a non-democratic set up countries; keep on ruling the public and serving their own interests in the name of benevolence/democracy; election after election; and thus the richer gets richer and the poor becomes poorer. In order to carry out their agenda they have strong holds on the points of their interest, as well as, the system through which they disguise their intended activities in the name of public's welfare/safety, country's interests, and so on.

These groups provide financial support to the; to be elected representatives, and political parties for advancing their cause and control the executives of these countries for their non humanly motives like Iraq War and so on at the public's expense and lives of these countries.

MINORITY AGENDA:

The politicians put forward their own chosen agenda and policies that they will carry out once elected in the wake of voters' restricted choice. No party has fought election on the basis of what the public generally wants that party to do if elected. The agenda or policies of political party in running, pertains to a very tiny minority who are rich/well educated running the party management directly; or indirectly in Europe, America and other developed countries, whereas, the less developed countries with rampant corruption, illiteracy have mostly illiterate democratic representative mustering support from the illiterate voters according to their area of influence whether it be by promising special favors or by buying the votes or bagging the votes by threatening the voters of dire consequences in the event of their failure to vote for their candidate.

The tiny minorities forwarding their self style agenda are found on both sides of the political arena that is with the ruling party, as well as, with the opposition bringing both sides to their point of common interests where the minority's interests are given priority. The minority has thus commanded influence on both sides i.e. for the government and opposition through the medium of print, radio, TV talk shows, ads, etc.

The general public of the country affected or to be affected by the policies designed by tiny minority which have no consideration for the general public, in alleviating their suffering whatever the conditions may be.

'Elections are held to dilute the populace into believing that they are participating in government". GERALD F. LIEBERMAN PAGE 82-3500

The general public is never asked to put forward their own agenda so that policies can be made and guided towards achieving the public's welfare.

PUBLIC MISPERCEPTION:

The few influential persons in the country like writers, speaker, lobbyists, etc. make their own deduction of public perception while staying in their circle of influence, according to their self designed agenda and questionnaires in total disregard and ignorance of the various conditions and states the public is actually in. These special groups use various kinds of influences to further their cause to name a few like super power influences, political influences, economical influence, psychological influence, social influence, religious influence and so on which are mostly exerted and supplemented by false propaganda, manipulated propaganda of connecting every bad omen with their intended target. These influential groups share common interests and goals around the world from across the continents and various countries as against the common interests of the society and country that they reside in. These groups are so very well organized that they start their activities well in advance of the decision of the voters, to influence their voting preference in their own favor, by media campaign. The media is normally controlled by them thus obliterating the other side of the story. The campaign issues are controlled and guided by these groups to achieve their intended target without any foreign or domestic opposition. There are aims and objectives to be achieved in remote countries at the cost of host country for the benefit of these interest groups. The public resources of the resident country in the shape of money and blood are used to cause bloodshed and destruction in target countries, to achieve the interest groups nefarious designs.

These special interest groups play on both sides of the bi-party and the multi-party country systems that is with the governing party/ parties and the opposition party/parties and use the representative of both parties in achieving their aims and thus are winners, no matter which party comes into power.

"The only thing we learn from new elections is we learned nothing from the old." (American proverb).PAGE#82-3500

VOTERS

How much of the general public is good and how much bad is a very good question because everybody is good to himself but at what expense i.e., at the expense of the others or to the benefit of others. In a simple context if the general public at large is bad (morally, socially, religiously, conduct wise etc.) the laws devised by their elected representative will be as bad: as against the general public which at large is good and the laws devised by the elected representative will be as good.

Now if the majority is bad then naturally the elected representative (from amongst themselves) will be as bad and when a bad person devises laws these will be as bad because he/she will deny justice to the righteous ones, will justify their bad conduct in a hook or crook manner, pass socially ill and evil laws, deny morality by hook or crook, go against the religion and religious beliefs to gain the votes, attain monetary benefits and social status in utter disregard of religious and natural laws prescribed by God All Mighty for the benefit and betterment of his creation in this world and the hereafter (CAN SINNERS BE THE WINNERS ?).

How do we distinguish between individuals whether they are good or bad the simple and golden rule is that one who helps others in need is good and one who puts them in difficulties is bad. People who work for the benefit of the majority are good and one's who work for their own selfish ends are bad.

"The Golden Rule has no place in a political campaign" (JOHN JAMES INGALLS).PAGE# 107-3500

The people who do good deeds are the best amongst the population of any country; the question arises as how do we recognize these people in the general public. Though it is a very good question but in the absence of our knowledge about inner motives of a person we can only judge a person by his/her conduct. That is to say if he/she deals fairly with others, is truthful, is honest, keeps his/her promises, does not blame others for the ill of the society, helps the needy and the poor, sides with justice against injustice, stands for the betterment of masses, society and country. Above all; reasons with all the pros and cons;

before reaching a decision instead of blindly following others and also stands up for the masses to alleviate their sufferings.

"Every creature alive lives by the Golden Rule, which they take to mean, get all the gold you can" 107-3500

THAILAND

Thailand provides us many lessons and explanations when we evaluate democracy and its effect, on the nations as against monarchy rule by a single person be he called a ruler, king, amir, etc. The democracy took effect in Thailand in 1992. Only two decades have passed and the results of democracy as described in the book are out, confirming the facts mentioned herein.

The nation is divided in two main factions as against the united nation of 1992. Democracy divided the nation's population as to literate vs illiterate; urban vs rural; proud vs lowly; establishment elite vs the poor/common individuals (economic division) while as Bill Tarrant describe the monarchy "REVERED KING – BHUMIBOL ADULYADET the only monarch most Thaïs have ever known and Thailand's unifying father figure," . According to Danny Richards, analyst of the Economist Intelligence Unit, "It could be difficult for the King to intervene without appearing to favor one side or the other, and their potentially compromising his authority as a parental figure dedicated to the well being of all Thai people". But there is also a very sad side to it that is the King's Advisors – Privy Council include ESTABLISHMENT ELITE'S former Premier – PREM TINSULANONDA and Army Chief – SURAYUD CHULANONT (it is alleged that he has illegal occupation of state forest) as members.

Bill Tarrant describes the divided nation, "Thailand's fundamental divide between the disenfranchised poor and what they call "ESTABLISHMENT ELITE" represents a collapse of a traditional order in Thailand at a time when people have begun to broach the hitherto taboo topic of succession".

According to Patrick Falby, "The reds complain that Thailand's poor have been left behind while the Bangkok middle class enjoy the fruits of decades of economic growth and the elites hold the rights of political and military power". Patrick Falby writes that according to the observers – Thailand, "is now heading into uncharted territory as a split deepens between its elites and the rural and urban poor".

The red's as described by Patrick Falby, "They are mostly supporters of ex-premier Thaksin Shinawatra, who was arrested in a 2006 coupe celebrated for populist policies that benefited the poor, Thaksin was also accused of gross lusma rights abuses and corruption. ------ Despite the criticism, Thaksin and his allies have won every election in a decade and Abhisit faces a tough fight in the next vote, due by end of 2011".

Gwynne Dyer corroborates and affirms Patrick Falbey's observations in his article "Thailand's a close call" and states, "Thailand has been a democracy since 1992, but Thaksin was the first politician to appeal directly to the interests of the rural poor rather than just bribe their local village headmen to deliver their votes. He promised them debt relief, cheap loans, better healthcare and he delivered. But that was not how the urban elite wanted their tax money spent.

The basic issue in dispute here is whether Thailand is really a democracy or not. If it is, then one way or other the red-shirts must get their way, for they represent a clear majority of Thais, and they were cheated of the government they chose. But there is no obvious way to get from here to there."

Thus the misrepresentation of the majority (anti-government) by the minority – (yellow shirts, pro-government) has led to violence and killing in violent street battles in Bangkok and according to Paul Chambers, senior research fellow at Heiddbery, "Opposing nibs become the norms and then democracy is simply a dream. Elected governments are a side show to opposing nibs".

Protester's (red shirts have been killed and wounded in hundreds and protester leader Nattawent Saikuar said, "We want the UN because we don't trust we will receive justice from organizations in Thailand". In the prevalent atmosphere of mistrust a top protester leader has urged the revered King to intervene in the crisis.

REF; DAWN- FRIDAY MAY 14, 2010: MONDAY MAY 17, 2010: FRIDAY MAY 21, 2010.

CHAPTER FOUR

DEMOCRACY DIVISION/RIVALRIES

CANDIDATE

The election in an area divides the community according to their choice of political party agenda in a bi-party/ multi-party countries, as well as, the voters' choice of candidate. The voters are divided according to their perception, preoccupation, knowledge and judgment of political party's leadership and candidates.

The successful candidates in an election representing the political parties divide the public of the constituencies, as well as, the country according to their choice of party agenda and other petty issues, in total disregard of the greater percentage of votes out of the total votes cast in any one party's favor.

The bi-party or multi-party countries practicing democratic system of government results in, division of families, communities, and nation, according to their choice of the political party. The bi-party countries divide the nation two ways whereas the voters and general public follow one or the other party according to their family traditions like the republican family stays republican and vote for republican candidate as their forefathers did likewise the democrats vote for democrats. The undecided voters and general public is the one who evaluate the candidates (whether be presidential or congress men) and the policies of the two parties and vote for the one most matches their choice. There are people in democratic countries who follow one party in blind faith of their party leader who formed the party and might have died ages ago or on the other hand oppose the rival party just for the sake of opposition without reasoning and evaluating the candidates and parties as to their conduct and performance.

In every nation the people who get represented in the legislature through the elected candidate are voters who voted for that candidate of the party whether in the government, opposition or coalition. The opposition parties have seldom been seen putting forward constructive criticism, however, mostly destructive criticism is delivered just for the sake of criticism to show their opposition and create-division/ rivalries.

Generally, there are two types of candidates one who creates considerable influence based upon his good conduct in the past and can get the majority votes without the support of political party that he/she represents; the other one, is the one, who is only recognized by political party he/she represents and gets the votes or wins the party seat only by his/her association with the party and its popularity due to either good governance or leadership or policies or performance, whatever the case may be.

A candidate once elected in the election automatically gets a mandate to represent the voters who voted him in, according to the constitution of the country, until the next election. Now once elected who does he/she represents, who does he/she works for are two totally different passions.

"The ruling passion, be it what it will, the ruling passion conquers reason still" (ALEXANDER FOPE).

There are persons who as elected representatives display good conduct by accepting responsibility when something goes wrong in their domain and offer their resignation at once, while on the other hand, there are the ones who stick to their seats in shame after something goes wrong in their domain displaying bad conduct and denying responsibility by shifting the onus on to others.

Then there are elected representatives who switch party allegiance, after the election, to get monetary and other benefits, in total disregard for the choice of party voters, who have voted him/her in as representative of that party. Since, the candidate has been elected by the constituency voters to represent the policies and carry on the mandate of the party platform that he/she contested elections on, and once he/she leaves that platform he/she is no longer the elected representative of his/her constituency voters who have elected him/her as a party candidate with their choice of agenda, unless, he/she ran as an independent backed by voters confidence to represent them as he/she deems fit.

"Never vote for the best candidate, vote for the one who will do the least harm." (FRANK DANE).PAGE#46-3500

"Now and then an innocent man is sent to legislature." (KIN HUBBARD).PAGE#183-3500

"In politics the choice is constantly between two evils." (JOHN MORLEY).PAGE#183-3500

"You don't have to fool all the people all of the time; you just have to fool enough to get elected." (GERALD BARZAN). PAGE#184-3500

POLITICAL PARTIES:

Amongst the countries running under democratic systems besides the totalitarian single party systems some of the countries have a bi-party political system, whereas, the others have a multi-party political system. The bi-party political systems divides the nations two ways, one party in the government and the other in opposition, while the multi-party political systems divides the nation in a multi-way who have division/rivalries amongst themselves and maintain control of their area especially in under developed countries, somewhere by force and at the other places by cooperation.

In a multi-party political system generally the majority parties are one or two, whereas, the minority parties cling to the majority parties for obtaining benefits for themselves and sometimes for their voters. In some cases, the majority party offers various benefits to the leaders and legislative members of these minority parties for obtaining legislature votes.

"No political party has exclusive patent rights on prosperity" (Franklin D. Roosevelt).PAGE#184-3500

In bi-party politics the issues are clear to the public and their decision making is easy as the public has to evaluate the issues two ways like good policy vs. bad policy or, yes vs. no or, you have it or you don't. Thus, the public of the country is divided two ways like good vs. bad, rich vs. poor, old vs. young, great vs. lowly, learned vs. ignorant, black vs. white, catholic vs. protestant and so on. Thus, the issues are divided two ways that is you have it or you don't, yes or no, accept or reject and so on thus the voters are divided according to their acceptance or rejection of issues by using their right to vote. Special interest groups like women's lib, gun control, groups watching their interests in the middle east and so on are the most effective in a bi-party system countries, where most of the time these groups support both parties of their concerned countries in one shape or the other in order to have the pie and cream, none the less whichever party wins.

These groups in a bi-party system countries have strong supporters in the ruling party, as well as, in the opposition party thus bringing both the parties in strong support for their causes/issue at the country level as well as forcing the other friendly countries through the presence of these interest groups in those countries to voice and support their cause at international level.

In multi-party countries, it is rather difficult for one party to have a clear majority or if it does it has more foes than friends as against bi-party countries. The special groups lose their influence considerably in multi-party countries, if associated with parties having weak electoral support, but no influence is lost if these groups are associated with the party having strong electoral support. In multi-party countries these special groups normally support the few like two to three parties who would get most electoral support as shown by advance polls conducted by these special groups and their controlling/captive media and audiences to convince the voters to go with the winners and avoid the losers; in total disregard of their consciousness and self respect.

In multi-party countries the election agenda and policies of the party are sometimes (when the party is not in majority) sacrificed to get to the avowed representation by joining with other parties to form the government. The agenda and policies of the government forming parties are shared on the basis of you lose something to gain something, thus partly sacrificing party agenda and policies for accommodating the other parties and their representatives in achieving partial success for their voters. Which are now partially misrepresented as these voters cast their votes against the party's given election agenda and policy.

The objectives and ideologies thus given up some times have a very drastic effect on the party's results in next election, according to the number of voters negatively affected during the current tenure of ruling party. The loss of agenda and policies of the majority party forming coalition could result in substantial losses, whereas, the minority party could have substantial gains in next election

The public of a country is divided into segments according to the numbers of political parties and this division/rivalry is so strong in some countries (mostly less developed) that it divides; the basic household members, communities, and so on that strong rivalries are created resulting in violence for the political control of their respective area/ riding.

Election after election some of the minority parties never win even any sizable minority seats to have any political effect on the policies of their government in any way, although they have lots of votes which are scattered in different areas/ridings without carrying any weight in an election, however, their party leaders do gain importance and status in the political arena of the country because of the number of votes they carry with them which could be used by any other political party loosing an election by low margin to gain seats in an election by forming election coalition strategy among both the parties.

Most of the communist countries experience governance through a single party system, whereas, countries like USA, UK, New Zealand, Uruguay, Bulgaria, Upper Volta and Kenya experience bi-party political system of governance having one majority party and the other minority party as opposition. On the other hand, most of the Europe, South America, Africa and some Asian countries experience governance in a multi-party political system of environment where the majority party rules alone or if needed in case of majority party not winning a majority rule with the help of other parties by forming a coalition.

DIVISION OF POPULATION / VOTERS BY SEX:

The political parties and candidates divide country on the basis of their sex by advancing the cause of women liberation, equality with men and so on to get the most female votes for their candidates. The public/voters are thus divided on the basis of their sex to get the most female votes under the ever increasing female population of the world. The division on the basis of sex divides even the most united families on the basis of sex thus the household is divided according to male/female choice of candidate/political party which advances their respective cause, in total disregard of very close and strong family ties and association.

DIVISION OF POPULATION / VOTERS BY LANGUAGE:

The political parties generally place a candidate speaking the language of their voters within an area or riding of high language concentration thus dividing the population of a country on the basis of language in order to attract and get their votes in an election. The political parties form agenda/policies for giving special attention and favors to voters, of a special language, to attract and get their votes in an election, be it in the form of grants for the promotion of that language, or promising to provide municipal and government services in their language, or by promising to introduce that language in the schools and so on thus dividing the population/voters on the basis of language. The public is divided language-wise like French vs. English, Punjabi vs. Pathans, Spanish vs. English, Punjabi vs. Sindhis where the voters favorite is one who speaks their own language thus other important national issues/policies become redundant and are not given any weight while voting for their own linguistic candidate to place him/her in an avowed representation against the better one (candidate, who might be fighting for the more benefit/welfare of the population as against the linguistic candidate). The language is and has remained a powerful divider of the voters under democratic system of elections in developing and developed countries alike, where, the issues are settled and voted on the basis of language irrespective of the fact whether they benefit the majority or not.

The contesting candidate divides the voters on the basis of the language and the one's speaking the candidates' language vote for him/her in a biased manner by preferring the language over the conduct and suitability of the candidate. Thus, the language over-rides the voters' choice to cast his/her vote for the right and deserving candidate.

The language plays most important role in voting as the voters are fearful of losing their identity (in a minority situation) on the basis of their language, as well as, fearful of its dilution by the injunction of people speaking other languages in their area/riding. Furthermore, when the people speaking a language are in minority they are fearful of any laws which may be made against their people so as to lose their strength on the basis of language.

India among the world has majority of multilingual people which are strong language oriented. They would like to cast their vote in an election for the candidate speaking their language, irrespective of his/her conduct, performance, education, experience, and party policies/agenda. The political parties in order to win the seat in an election put forward a candidate in the area/riding who speaks the voters language and is likely to get the most votes on the basis of the language irrespective of his/her conduct education and experience (like Spanish in USA, French in Canada and so on).

DIVISIONS/RIVALRIES RACES/CASTS:

The public of a country is divided as to their races/casts where some consider themselves to be superior to others. The most diverse and a vast majority of races/casts are found in the Indian subcontinent on the one hand and to count a few on the other hand in England like The English, The Scottish, and The Irish and so on. Races/casts plays an important role in gathering votes from the people of the same race/cast irrespective of the candidates conduct, education, experience, political party policies/agenda he/she represents. The profile of the people of the same races/cast is very important for the success or failure of a candidate in an area/riding because the people of the same cast/race if united on one hand to make a candidate succeed could also be strong rivals of each other within a cast/race to let the same candidate to a defeat. The level of support to a considerable extent then depends upon the divisions/rivalries among the same race/cast unless the issue takes a form where the whole race will be let down if they did not make their own races/cast candidate succeed.

"The struggle of the black race to show that, if given the chance, it can screw up as good as the white race." FRANK DANE. PAGE#198-3500

DIVISIONS/RIVALRIES RELIGIONS/SECTS:

The religion forms the basic belief of the nation / communities / individuals for their conduct among each/other. The religion is further sub-divided into various sects carrying on and following the sect/cult leaders under the umbrella of their religion. People of different religions and sects in order to keep their jobs and their sect to be given a voice and importance want their own candidates to succeed in an election or else they vote for the candidate who tolerates / supports their sect / religion.

The three major religions commanding the population of the world in various countries as people of the book are Muslims, Christians, and Jews.

The majority of people without the book of God like India, China, Russia, Japan, Thailand, Burma, etc. have totally different considerations as to their basic belief as against the people of the book, Hindu theology divides its followers according to the theological cast system which is the root cause of dividing people instead of uniting them. The society is divided into segments according to the Hindu theology which starts at one end with the most respectable (Barhamans) and ends at other end as the Untouchables.

DIVISION/RIVALRY FOR ACQUISITION OF ECONOMIC RESOURCE:

The public is divided universally as to rich against poor, rich countries against poor countries, as well as, by fiscal and social systems prevailing to stabilize and balance the economic conditions through fiscal and monetary measures.

The public of the countries of the world is divided on the basis of their fiscal preferences as the rich would prefer no extra taxes at their higher end of income level while the average and poor would like to shift the burden of taxation towards the rich, and the poor would like to get the extra benefits and help from the government in the shape of income support, social assistance, etc.

The public of a country (like Sudan is divided in to two countries for the control of oil resources) is divided as to exploitation of resources in a country from one region to the benefit of other region.

Let us not forget the traditional division of the rich against poor which has resurfaced in many countries of the world and has over-turned tyrant and autocratic regimes not delivering the due benefits to their population like Tunisia, Egypt and Libya to begin with.

DIVISION/RIVALRY OF POPULATION RURAL VERSUS URBAN:

This is a very important aspect of division of population among almost all the countries of the world which is commonly given less weight or is ignored or put at the back, to be considered as least important. The rural and urban population has a very clear and broad distinction among the general population of a country. The rural population is generally associated with agriculture as against city dwellers associated with industries, services, transportation, finance, and so on. The rural population does not have much differences as to their occupation and day to day activities, whereas, the urban population have wide variety of non homogenous activities thus not providing a common platform to the politicians i.e., the political parties and candidates.

There are a wide variety of factors associated with the urban and rural groups from country to country. The less developed countries have up to 80% of the population living in rural areas associated with agriculture. This rural population has very low level of education and generally has limited access to the amenities and services as against the urban population. Both these groups have uncommon and conflicting priorities amongst each other as the rural group is associated with agriculture and urban group with industry, trade, commerce, transportation services and so on. The rural population is generally laborious associated with agriculture production. In developed countries, this group stands united to forward their cause of subsidies for agriculture inputs and outputs, whereas, in developing countries, people stand alone and gather around the renowned candidates on the basis of their cast and creed, and acquire basic services like electrification, schooling, water and drainage services, roads, etc. as well as following their elders to vote for the candidate of their choice who can side with them against their rivals in legal and other routine and non routine issues.

In the developing/developed countries election issues are generally nationwide like agricultural subsidies etc., whereas, in less developed countries the election issues are diverse starting at local level/village level. In the developing/developed countries, most of the rural vote goes with the party that promises to meet the farmers (who are very well organized) demands of subsidies etc. However, in less-developed countries,(the rural voters are not organized around the national issues) the basic issues as discussed above revolve around infrastructure in general, as well as, helping the farmers get along with the district/tehsil administration when needed. In less-developed countries the agricultural community in general is not organized and united in furthering their cause of price stability for agricultural inputs and outputs and the buyers/sellers, traders and hoarders, get most of the benefits in selling the agricultural inputs to the farmers and buying agricultural outputs from farmers at lower than normal rate thus getting most of the price spread benefits at the expense of farmers.

DIVISION OF POPULATION BY AGE:

The public is divided age wise as the old age group is generally against change in their customs, whereas, the middle aged group want job protection and secure future and the young generation wants jobs. Thus, the voters are divided age wise and the candidates in order to attract most votes go with the demands of the age group which would cast most votes in his/her favor and the other age groups will relatively be neglected as to their demands and issues.

The old people if commanding majority votes would not like to change the existing set up for the benefit of the other age groups to which they are conveniently accustomed. They will show a strong opposition towards changing the laws for other age groups which are not consistent with their old customs. One can conveniently suggest that any country's demography having majority of old people stick with their old and existing laws.

In Europe and North America the old age group especially the retired and senior citizens are solid votes with the highest turnover at the polls for the candidates of a party, who provide them with their choice of agenda/ benefits as the old age segment has steady growth of voters.

DIVISION OF POPULATION ON THE BASIS OF PROUD VS LOWLY:

Every country is strongly divided between these two kinds of public/voters. The proudly one's are the ones who are arrogant, unreasonable, rigid, oppressors and non sharing due to race, religion, wealth, descent, education, etc. The lowly ones are the humble, reasonable, flexible, tolerant and above all the best among the public of a country irrespective of race religion, wealth, descent, education etc. This division is not brought into open but is so strong underneath the skins to divide the nations (like Thailand) and is an open secret.

DIVISION OF POPULATION ON THE BASIS OF COLOR:

The public/voters are divided by color which plays a very important role where the chances of success are bright for the black candidate in a black riding, for the white candidate in white riding, and for the yellow candidate in yellow riding and so on.

Deprivation of color minorities by the white majority is a very common and focal point making these minorities feel deprived and neglected thus dividing the public/voters according to their color.

OVERTHROWN REGIMES – TUNISIA – EGYPT – LIBYA:

Mohammed Bauazizi a vegetable seller in Tunisian City of Sidi Bouzid ignited the revolution by setting himself on fire to lodge his protest against the repressive government of deposed dictator (for 23 year) Zine-al-Abidine Ben Ali who later fled to Saudi Arabia and took political asylum. The wave of unrest spread like fire to other Arab Countries bringing down the governments of Tunisia – Egypt and Libya having widespread poverty, unemployment and repressive governments. The governments of Tunisia and Egypt were brought down by the inside struggle with moral support provided by the foreign countries, whereas, the military might of America and Europe came to the National Transitional Forces support by providing arms to them and lodging a bombing campaign against Gaddafi and his forces because it is an oil producing country. The former two were called democracy movements, whereas, the Libyan revolt took the shape of National Transitional fighting forces.

Husani Mubarik ruled Egypt after the death of President Sadat as leader of the National Democratic Party as an autocrat/dictator. Gaddafi ruled Libya for 42 years less 8 days after he was injured and killed by the National Transitional forces in an inhuman way. The human rights organizations want his brutal murder to be investigated and the responsible ones for this inhumanly act to be punished for their barbaric action.

REF; DAWN FRIDAY MARCH 4, 2011—WEDNESDAY JUNE 8, 2011. FRIDAY SEPTEMBER 30, 2011. OCTOBER 25, 2011. THE NATION SUNDAY OCTOBER 2, 2011.

SYRIA

Syria is heading towards somewhat formation of armed groups joined by the Syrian military deserters especially those personnel who refused to open fire on civilian public protestors. The arms are being smuggled for the protestors through neighboring countries, whereas, Asad regime has accused Washington of inciting armed groups into violence against its army, and these armed groups and unarmed protestors are serving foreign goals against the interests of the Syrian public. Asad regime has sought to crush the pro-democracy movement that has shaken his regime in an unprecedented manner by killing more than 2700 protestors by the end of September, 2011 in total disregard of dialogue/negotiations. The protestors in Syria have slogan "victory for our Syria and victory for our Yemen".

BAHRAIN

The agitations and protests continue in the country where the majority of Shiites are being ruled by Sunni minority.

Bahrain has Shia Muslim majority which is governed by Sunni Al-Khalifa dynasty. Protests erupted in the kingdom after Ali was killed by police outside his house in February, 2011 led by Shia community demanding an end to sectarian discrimination and a greater say in the government, King Hamad Bin Isa al-khalifa although has made conciliatory statements; he has squashed the protests in March, 2011 with the help of troops from Saudia Arabia and the United Arab Emirates. The Shia population has a political party al-wifaq led by Ali Salman.

YEMEN

President Ali Abdullah Saleh has ruled Yemen for the last 33 years. The Gulf Cooperation Council (GCC) has taken initiative to end the Yemen Crisis. The UN Security Council has passed resolution 2014 backing the Gulf peace plan which will provide immunity to

President Ali Abdul Saleh to sign a deal to step down in exchange for immunity. Saleh's conduct is like an open book whereby he has already backed down three times from signing the gulf initiative which came after months of protests; and Saleh's three times backing down has resulted in more deaths and destruction that he is solely responsible for, therefore, the world immunity in case of hundreds of deaths or even one intentional death anywhere in the world is a misnomer which misleads the reader and obstructs the justice to the victim under any international/local laws around the world.

REF; DAWN MARCH 4, 2011.SEPTEMBER 30, 2011. OCTOBER 01, 2011. OCTOBER 05, 2011. THE "NEWS", SEPTEMBER 09, 2011. THE NATION OCTOBER 02, 2011.

IRAQ

REF; DAILY TIMES OCTOBER 23, 2011.

Iraq was invaded by United States in 2003 for interests that ranged from revenge to capturing oil resources and destroy its fighting forces which was obviously a big threat to the neighbors of Iraq; friendly to the United states. Bush administration invaded Iraq to topple Saddam Hussain against false and fake propaganda that he had weapons of mass destruction. The US occupation of Iraq is expected to end in December, 2011 as announced by President Obama.

SUDAN

REF; DAWN FRIDAY OCTOBER 07,2011
REF; THE NEWS OCTOBER 09,2011

Sudan was divided into Sudan and Southern Sudan on July 9, 2011. The country was divided over oil resources. Sudanese conflict has lead to a large loss of life, injured and displaced persons than Libya, Tunisia and Egypt combined. The now independent Southern Sudan further faces the threat of internal divisions which could lead to more independent states in future.

The breakaway state of Southern Sudan produces three quarters of Sudan's total crude output of 470,000 barrels per day, oil exports of South Sudan account for 95% of its total revenue.

Sudan provides to the Southern Soudan oil infrastructure including refinery, pipelines and export facilities for which it wants to charge $32 per barrel for facility usage.

THIS 'DEMOCRACY' IS NOT ENOUGH BY AMEER BHUTTO:

The several Arab rulers bearing the brunt of public wrath, a number of our parliamentarians have recently appeared on television talk shows to pre-empt a similar fate by mocking and condemning public political activism. They say that it has become fashionable, since the success of the lawyers movement, to try to settle all scores in the streets. They argue that there is no need for such extreme measures in the presence of an elected parliament. Have they forgotten that they are sitting in parliament and enjoying the perks of power only by virtue of the mandate issued to them by the public? Who are they to preach complacent inaction to the people when they have failed to solve their problems? The people are the political sovereign. They are the fount of political legitimacy and authority. Their role in the democratic process does not end at the polls, nor is their mandate a carte blanche for rulers to run amok and unchecked for a whole term. It is constant and continuous public scrutiny that keeps governments honest in western democracies.

Far from limiting the role of the public, there is an urgent need for greater public awareness and involvement, because the ship of state is floundering and needs to be rescued. We need a salvage operation which only the people care about and are capable of carrying out. Some reject this outright because their political survival depends on the status quo and are busy making hay while the sun shines. Others are of the view that Pakistan cannot be bracketed with the Middle Eastern countries because the scenario here is different.

They argue that, unlike Middle Eastern states, we have democracy. Do we? Where is it? Elections alone do not define democracy. There was an elected parliament and president in Egypt. Should a government of the people for the people and by the people' not be founded on a genuine and palpable commitment to serve the people particularly those in desperate need, rather than feathering its own nest? Is duping the people by begging for votes in the name of a slain leader and then letting her killers walk scot-free after forming a government democracy? Is stabbing political allies in the back democracy? Is sacrificing public and national interests at the altar of expediency before foreign masters' democracy? Is record-breaking corruption and sleaze that has rubbed national pride and honor in the mud all over the world democracy? Do democratic leaders take off to visit chateaus in France or for a sojourn in the presidential suite at the Churchill Hotel in London, while their country is drowning in the worst flood in nearly a hundred years? Does democracy condone a daily budget of 2.5 million rupees for the presidential and prime ministerial palaces while, even six months after the floods, the displaced refugees continue to die from starvation and bitter cold in camps? How can anyone gloat about this 'democracy' that, far from empowering the people and serving their interests, exacerbates and compounds their pain and misery? It is worse that some of the Arab monarchies and dictatorships the people are striving to over-throw.

We have had six general elections since 1988. Has the lot of the common man improved by even an iota since then? While those who have wielded power in this period have prospered enormously, with some who used to travel in buses and live in mud shacks having acquired fleets of luxurious vehicles and palatial properties not just in Pakistan but all over the world, the poor laborer and hari has been pushed into such desperation that he must sell his children to make ends meet. It may seem politically correct to extol the virtues of this lame 'democracy' and peddle ridiculous and meaningless clichés like the worse democracy is better than the best dictatorship' on talk shows and in plush drawing rooms, but go to the villages and inner cities where people are losing daily battles for survival and tell them that they are better off under this 'democracy' and see what they do.

It is said that unlike the troubled Arab states, important state institutions in Pakistan are independent and can be instrumental in resolving issue of public importance. If this is the case, then why are people out in the streets, with dozens of protests and demonstrations taking place all over the country every day? Yes, parliament is elected and empowered to provide relief to the people, but their greatest achievements thus far has been the sanctioning of construction of new residences for themselves at a cost of three billion rupees, while people are committing suicides daily because of hunger and poverty. In what way has parliament lessened the agony that people endure every day? Yes, the judiciary is finally free and is in the vanguard of the fight against this government's corruption and illegal conduct, but the government has found an easy way around it by simply ignoring its orders. If the courts push harder for the implementation of their orders, they are accused of judicial activism. Yes, the media is independent, but all they can do is report realities. They cannot remedy the problems. All important state agencies and institutions have been put under the control of government thugs to facilitate loot and plunder. NAB, under its new chairman, has reportedly withdrawn cases in which over 61 billion rupees were allegedly embezzled. How does this help the cause of the people or the country?

It is argued that the current dispensation in Pakistan is not despotic, in the sense that Qaddafi's is in Libya. But there are other ways to inflict pain and suffering on a nation. Record-breaking corruption that leeches the life blood out of the state, horrifying incompetence, ignorance and malicious intent that have ground all public institutions to a halt and gross negligence that is eroding the edifice of state all combine to have the same excruciating effect as despotism; the people are denied resources that should be earmarked for their uplift, they have no security of life, property and dignity and continue to be squeezed by the claws of poverty and lack of opportunity, education, health services, electricity and clean water with no relief in sight.

If a chasm so wide opens up between the people and the government, if a government strays so far from its mandate and obligations, does it not become the moral duty of the people to step forward and correct the anomaly when the system clearly cannot? In Pakistan, we need to go beyond targeting just one leader, one party or a failed, useless, indeed harmful, government. The whole system has collapsed because it has been made hollow by repeated perversions. It needs not just a jolt, but reconstruction.

However, there are no portents of the needed public uprising on the horizon. That does not mean that it is not needed or that it should not or cannot happen. It is undeniably desperately needed and will happen. But its beginnings are not visible at the moment. This is so because despite continuous intolerable pain and humiliation, people habitually sell out too cheaply, for a watan card or a thousand rupees handout from the Benazir Income Support Scheme. The authorities in Egypt tried to buy people off by announcing similar handouts, but it did not work. We should learn a lesson from them. But the beautiful thing about revolutions is that they happen when least expected. Nobody could have predicted the uprising in Tunisia even weeks before it happened. Why should it be considered an impossibility here where it is needed more urgently?

The writer is vice-chairman of the Sindh National Front and a former MPA from Ratodero. He has degrees from the University of Buckingham and Cambridge University. Courtesy, " The News" – Dated: March 05,2011.

OUR SICKLY DEMOCRACY BY BABAR SATTAR:

In the absence of a functional democracy rooted in constitutionalism and rule of law, is it surprising that civilian control of the military remains elusive in Pakistan? "The wonder… is not why the military rebels against its civilian masters, but why it ever obeys them," asserted Samuel Finder in his seminal work 'The man on the horseback'. Students of civil-military relations continue to squabble over the allocation of blame to adventurist khakis and non-performing civilian regimes for the breakdown of democracy. Whether one believes that an over-bloated military keeps democracy weak and dysfunctional by design to guard its turf and create opportunities to assume greater control of the state, or that corrupt and ineffectual political regimes create a vacuum that the khakis are forced to fill, there is agreement that a dysfunctional civilian government partly explains military intervention.

Last week, speaking to officers of Quetta Staff College, the Chief Justice of Pakistan reminded khakis that the principle of civilian control of the military was firmly rooted in the Constitution. He candidly recounted our past for their benefit. "The history of Pakistan reflects a recurring conflict between underdeveloped a political system and a well-organized army. When there are political crises, we have witnessed military intervention followed by military rule. Thus, there emerged a vicious circle of brief political dispensation followed by prolonged military rule. This state of affairs brought many setbacks and hampered the process of evolution of constitutionalism and the democratic system of governance. He also reiterated the concept of equality before law by reminding the officers that, "the soldier and the citizen stand alike under law... both must obey the command of Constitution and show obedience to its mandate."

The khakis must not view the Constitution as a useless scripture. It would do this country a whole lot of good if they revisited their sociology and made allegiance to our fundamental law part of their conception of professionalism. But there has never been much dispute about what the military ought to do from a constitutional perspective. Yet one bleeding heart dictator after another has told us that the skies are about to cave in and if the generals don't follow their self-assumed obligation (in conflict with dictates of law) to step in and save the nation, we are all doomed. We blame judges for abetting dictators and conjuring up legal fiction for the purpose, as we should. But even if they were to abide by their oath to protect the Constitution and go down fighting, as they must, would it prevent military interference in politics?

This is no apology for the loathsome doctrine of necessity. But will generals suddenly see the light, start taking their oath of allegiance to the Constitution seriously and yield to civilian control. Notwithstanding whether one lays the blame for military takeovers on power hungry generals or blundering political elite, the opportunity to intervene in politics will not dry up unless a democratic system of governance delivers, political parties emerge as representative institutions, politics is focused on policy making and not power grab alone, and political culture accommodates integrity, dissent and merit. We can continue to cry conspiracy, but so long as dividends of democracy do not trickle down to the ordinary citizen, the polity will remain vulnerable to generals lurking in the shadows.

Pakistan: Beyond the 'Crisis State' edited by Dr. Maleeha Lodhi and recently published is recommended reading for anyone interested in finding solutions to the myriad problems confronting us as a nation-state. It addresses the whole gamut of issues holding up our potential ranging from myopic ideology, skewed foreign policy, tenuous economy and civil-military imbalance to the crisis of energy and education. Given that the contributors are not foreigners, the analysis, critique, solutions, frustrations and hope that it presents are indigenous. Members of our elites (especially political elites) who view themselves as agents of progression and change would do well to read the book and especially the chapter authored by Dr. Lodhi.

Undemocratic party structures, a feudal-tribal culture, and politics of patronage as opposed to policy are three of the main weaknesses identified by Dr. Lodhi that create a disconnect between civilian government and public service. Presently, there is no separation between political party as an institution and its top leadership. In the absence of institutional autonomy or shared decision-making, the policies of the party are essentially the whims of its leader. The barriers to entry and upward progression within parties prevent them from grooming leaders and nurturing the talent, ideas and expertise required to run a government.

The institutional deficiencies are compounded by the power elites' feudal-tribal' style of conducting politics that fuels sycophancy and shuns dissent, and is described by Dr. Lodhi as, "personalized, based on 'primordial' social hierarchies, characterized by patronage seeking activity and preoccupied with protecting and promoting their economic interests and privileged status." Such autocratic party structure and political culture directs the focus of politics toward acquiring the spoils of office to reward 'clients' and buttress traditional networks of patronage and political support, as opposed to seeking public office to implement policies and improve the system of governance for the benefit of all citizens.

We saw Benazir Bhutto gift her father's party to her son through a will. We see Shahbaz Sharif's son being treated as heir apparent of the PML-N. We witness Asif Zardari, Nawaz Sharif, Asfandyar Wali, Fazalur Rehman, Altaf Hussain and the Chaudharies lord over their respective parties on an everyday basis. There is no room for dissent within political parties. Be it Aitzaz Ahsan, Shah Memood Qureshi or Safdar Abbasi of the PPP or Javed Hashmi of the PML-N, any independent thinking amounts to disloyalty, attracts the ire of the party leader and clips the dissenter's role within the party.

Javed Hashmi exhibited tremendous character when he expressed shame for supporting a dictator two and half decades back. He showed remarkable courage when he called upon the Sharifs to assume responsibility for past choice and actions. Would Nawaz Sharif not emerge as a bigger man if he took Javed Hashmi's advice and apologized to the nation for being a part of the Zia regime? And do members of the PPP who celebrated Mr. Hashmi's speech in the National Assembly, not see the hypocrisy in their perfect ease with Asif Zardari treating the PPP as his personal fief?

Do they not realize that given the ideology, manifesto and political program of the PPP, their party has nothing in common with the PML-Q, except the shared desire of their respective leaders to distribute the spoils of office amongst themselves and their cronies?

Democracy is more than a process. Its pith and substance is system of governance that protects and serves the interests of ordinary citizens, regardless of their political preferences. It is in upholding the substance of democracy that ineffectual civilian governments falter and as a consequence cede political space to generals. While uninterrupted political process is imperative to realize the dividends of democracy, public support for such continuity cannot be fostered by a ruling political elite visibly un-responsive to public needs.

The message of hope springing out of Pakistan: Beyond the Crisis State is the inevitability of change being ushered in by a growing, informed and assertive middle class together with a free and vocal media. Pakistan is not ready to suffer another, khaki savior. But neither is it willing to put up indefinitely with autocratic civilian regimes engaged in a transaction relationship with ordinary people, reducing them to petty clients. Business, as usual, is not longer sustainable. Political parties can either become vehicles for change or get wiped away as agents of the status quo.

Email: sattar@post.harvard.eduCOURTSEY **The" News" Saturday April 30, 2011.**

CHAPTER FIVE

MISREPRESENTATION

POPULATION MISREPRESENTATION IN AN ELECTION:

The elected representative represent's what percentage of population of his/her constituency/riding? In due consideration of election logic the candidate represents simple majority if he/she gets more votes than the rival candidates contesting in the area/riding or else if looser he/she represents minority.

"We go by the major vote, if the majority is insane, the same must go to the hospital" (HORCE MANN)PAGE#144-3500

"The majority is always wrong; the minority is rarely right." (HENRIK IBSEN)PAGE#144-3500

The eligible voters in different countries are the one who have attained a certain age as specified under the constitution, to be registered, and are registered as voters. Generally in most countries, the eligible voters are citizens of that country who have attained the age of 18 years' whereas in some countries it is 21 years.

The population of a country, less than 18 years/21 years of age, varies according to the choice of married couples regarding their family size. Therefore, the population not eligible to vote; and those that are not represented for electing a political candidate in an election, might range from 20% to 40% of the total population of a country depending upon the family composition in various countries practicing democratic system of government.

This segment of the population which is not being represented besides the percentage of voters that do not take part in an election, is the most important, whose future is being put in jeopardy or is being laden with debt/or being made hazardous by nuclear plants/bombs or the environment being made hostile due to the present government hostilities towards other countries/or being made economically unsound/or being made difficult and in most cases most difficult by lavishly enjoying/wasting the available natural resources by the present population in total disregard of future generations.

Thus the segment of the population not represented in an election will be affected most in future by the present government policies, not tailored towards the future generations, who have not been counted/ or given importance/or left out because they were not the voters in the current election.

The future voters who are unable to cast their votes at present because they were not eligible voters are not given any importance by the political parties and candidates as they do not at all affect the outcome of the election. This future generation is thus totally devoid of the opportunities/potential they would realize if counted/considered/ and involved in the decision-making process of political arena. Since this population of unregistered voters is of no use to the political party candidates contesting election, this future generation of voters is totally ignored as to their present and future needs and requirements. On the other hand, the same future generation is being overburdened with debt, and they have to pay back the same by paying heavy taxes in future for which they have not availed any benefits.

MISREPRESENTATION OF POPULATION BY VOTERS FORMING SPECIAL INTEREST GROUPS.

The elected representatives of a political party and their leadership accommodate, voters forming special groups, like abortionists, gay/lesbian movement, 'freedom to carry' guns- movement, and so on against the moral and ethical values of society. These very well-organized special groups also provide financial support to the political parties through various organizations and industries for making derogatory laws against humanity along with launching a media campaign to convince the public to accept the wrong as right and right as wrong. The financial support provided to the respective political party causes the elected member to return the favor by putting up and voting for the derogatory laws. These laws infringe upon the rights of general public at large and some groups and industries in specific as these special groups were unable to get the control of these groups and industries for their own benefit. In some cases, the benefits to the general public are not brought up explicitly and in full detail instead the costs are inflated to show the losses/sufferings to the general public at large.

Blasphemous laws like gay marriages are passed which ends the human race if followed by everybody then there is abortion being made from illegal to legal which is tantamount to murdering the human race again if followed by everybody concerned. Then there are laws restricting the freedom of human beings to smoke in public under the disguise of public health being spoiled by smoking in public, whereas, on the other hand, billions of vehicles and numerous industries all over the world are emitting carbon dioxide/monoxide which makes almost one third of the world population suffering from respiratory related illnesses in addition to causing the global warming. When we compare the respiratory illnesses with smoking there are more deaths (approximately 800,000 in 2013) caused by respiratory related illnesses due to the pollutants emitted by vehicles and industries than by human beings smoking in public; and even more deaths caused by people driving while intoxicated. Smoking in this hectic world soothes the nerves of the smokers and saves the society of many evils worse than smoking like fights, separation of marriages and so on however, addiction of any kind is bad and harmful for the addicts.

The negative/unnatural laws made against the religious spirit and beliefs of public at large whether these be Jews, Christians, and Muslims, to accommodate the people who have financially supported the political parties and have provided the votes of their groups/communities to the political party candidates in an election against the religious beliefs of the majority, and in some cases to vent their anger against the industries for which they were not able to acquire controlling interests by placing legal restrictions on these industries through their influence on avowed representatives that they have financially supported for devising and passing restrictive legislation in one form or another, or in some cases closing down these industries by misstating the facts that cannot be proved, as well as, by the use of only one side of the story being stated by their controlled friendly media.

The above commentary was necessary to make a point that the legislators play into the hands of few against their voters choice, who have provided financial support to these legislators and their political parties; and this support is recouped by many folds over by these few making these few richer and ever richer at the cost of lost benefits to the general public; by devising and making laws for the benefit of the few to extort money from the majority of general public; to name two from among the long list like the auto insurance industry(where monthly insurance payments are almost equal to the payments made to automakers for the vehicle can the politicians tell the public as to, how many vehicles the insurance firms replace/make every month against the total premiums paid to them? as the same politicians have forced insurance slavery on the public through insurance act) , health industry emptying the pockets of the general public for the benefit of the few – whereas general public already have great difficulty in making their ends meet.

This is one kind of legal extortion where the companies (providing financial help to the political parties are allowed (like insurance industry, health industry and so on) to rip the general public off, under the compulsion of laws made upon the influence of the few (against the agenda and policies of the party) to extort the money out of the general public which is already burdened with heavy taxation for the benefit of these few influential goons.

Money from the public kitty for their own benefit also influence and convince the politicians to fight their wars, with the public's lives and there are some of these special interest groups besides extorting money, to achieve their own inner agenda, like running their arms/ammunition industries as well as to vent their anger against the militarily weak and sovereign countries who do not take dictation from them, by waging war against them and in the end getting themselves defeated as against defeating the so called enemy which is weak but is shown as strong (totally against the all open evidence like military, and economic facts) by facts which are blown out of proportion (in the light of their spy agencies working around the clock) to turn the true facts to fiction. Thus, these special interest groups indulge the countries and public in wars across the continents to make money, control the resources of other countries, and achieve their inner motives through the use of your (the voters) tax money and lives, as you the voters and your families have ultimately been fighting for their causes and their wars; as against none of their own just cause and benefit. Thus the wealth of the nation transferred to these groups and lives are lost, for a lost cause whereas, you are further plunged into recession with unemployment and then to depression with mass unemployment and bankruptcies, for the sake of others – who are few – that you have made them rich and powerful – and have provided your own control in their hands through the ballot box once in four to five years as the case may be. Thus, the rich get's richer and continues to press these destructive policies for nations for their own good.

Then there are other special groups who have supported the political parties through votes on the conditions of making legislation for their cause like the environment groups, hunting groups, groups against restriction on arms and ammunition for the general public. These groups push through legislation laws for furthering and advancing their own cause without due consideration of its impact on general public of the country.

MISREPRESENTATION OF VOTERS BY THE ELECTED CANDIDATE:

The candidate elected in an election misrepresents the voters, if the election is not free, fair, and transparent. Bogus votes have been cast by the party stooges. There are ghost polling stations resulting in Ballot boxes full of bogus votes.

The candidate elected in an election misrepresents the voters when he/she changes his/her political party after being elected in an election since, the voters have voted him/her in on the basis of the political party policies and agenda that he/she contested election on.

The candidate elected in an election misrepresents the voters after the political party that he/she contested election on do not follow their pre-election agenda and policies, then the elected candidate has a right to quit the political party and represent his/her electoral by switching to the party that closely matches the voters choice of agenda and policies or on the other hand resign and let the voters re-choose him under the changed political party agenda/policies.

The candidate elected in an election misrepresents the voters when he/she starts working after being elected not for the interests of the voters/constituents but for the interests of groups other than voters, organizations or business against his/her oath of office for fair representation of the voters/constituents.

The candidate elected in an election from a constituency sides with the voters of his choice by discriminating against the other constituent voters that have also voted him/her in, thus misrepresenting the voters that have voted him/her in the avowed representation.

MISREPRESENTATION OF VOTERS BY THE POLITICAL PARTY:

The political parties misrepresent their voters who have voted in their candidates from their respective constituencies when the pre-election agenda and policies that their members received votes on, are not followed by the political parties who when elected and in power start following their own personal interests driven by the interest groups other than voters.

The onus of responsibility falls on party elected members if they side with the party leadership when the pre-election agenda and policies are not followed and if they do not side with the party leadership when the pre election agenda and policies are followed by the party. The party leadership is also responsible for the agenda and policies against the voter's choice.

Generally, in a democratically elected party leadership there is not much chance of the party leadership to go against the wishes of the voter's, however, in a dictatorial form of party leadership there is a greater chance of the party leadership going against the wishes of the voters who have put that party in the governing seat.

In both of the above cases that is the members as well as leadership, the oaths of office are violated-neglected, the morality is replaced with immorality, the voters and the country's interest is foregone for the benefits of the party's elected membership and the party leadership.

The elected party membership; which only represents the party members that have voted them in and not the population of the country; when start representing the third party interests be it in the form of a dictator party leader, or other interest groups; misrepresentation and violation of oath kicks in, in which case morality dictates that he/she should resign.

M E D I A:

I quote "It was the British election biggest media but-up. After the Independent launched an advertising campaign with the slogan "Rupert Murdoch Won't decide this election --- you will" and "The Murdoch papers backed the Tories, the standard backs the Tories too, while the new Indy urged its readers to vote for the Liberal Democrats in a bid to secure electoral reform."

Luke Harding writes about Labelers (owner of three British newspapers London evening, Standard Independent and Independent on Sunday, "latest big Idea is to establish an international agency that works collaboratively on investigation, and is staffed by journalists from leading newspaper titles around the world. The agency would investigate topics such as global corruption, the oil industry and the abuse of offshore trusts," and Labeler describes his journalistic ambitions, "The number one element if you are a journalist which I hope to become one day, is that you put everything in doubt".

Lube Harding further writes about the financial condition of Lebeder, "offer is locked in a legal battle with German partner of his bankrupted airlines business, Blue Wings.

His London – listed oil company, Timan Oil & Gas, meanwhile, also faces liquidation after its Russian Manager allegedly stripped the firm of all its assets. Labeler says he has lost EUR 290 M on Blue Wings and $ 20 M from the doomed oil venture".

REF; DAWN MAY 17, 2010.

AMERICA'S NEW AFRICAN EMPIRE
BY PAUL CRAIG ROBERT
WILL THE US COLLAPSE IN ECONOMIC CHAOS BEFORE IT RULES THE WORLD?

Now that the CIA's proxy army has murdered Gaddafi; what next for Libya?

If Washington's plans succeed, Libya will become another American puppet state. Most of the cities, towns and infrastructure have been destroyed by air strikes by the air forces of the US and Washington's NATO puppets. U.S and European firms will now get juicy contracts, financed by US taxpayers, to rebuild Libya. The new real estate will be carefully allocated to lubricate a new ruling class picked by Washington. This will put Libya firmly under Washington's thumb.

With Libya conquered, AFRICOM will start on the other African countries where China has energy and mineral investments. Obama has already sent US troops to Central Africa under the guise of defeating the Lord's Resistance Army, a small insurgency against the ruling dictator-for-life. The Republican Speaker of the House, John Boehner, welcomed the prospect of yet another war by declaring that sending US troops into Central Africa "furthers US national security interests and foreign policy." Republican Senator James Inhofe added a gallon of moral verbiage about saving "Ugandan children," a concern the senator did not have for Libya's children or Palestine's, Iraq's, Afghanistan's and Pakistan's.

With Libya conquered, AFRICOM will start on the other African countries where China has energy, and mineral investments. Obama has already sent US troops to Central Africa under the guise of defeating the Lord's Resistance Army, a small insurgency against the ruling dictator-for-life.

Washington has revived the Great Power Game and is vying with China. Whereas China brings Africa investment and gifts of infrastructure, Washington sends troops, bombs and military bases. Sooner or later Washington's aggressiveness toward China and Russia is going to explode in our faces.

Where is the money going to come from to finance Washington's African Empire? Not from Libya's oil. Big chunks of that have been promised to the French and British for providing cover for Washington's latest war of naked aggression. Not from tax revenues from a collapsing US economy where unemployment, if measured correctly, is 23 percent.

With Washington's annual budget deficit as huge as it is, the money can only come from the printing press.

Washington has already ran the printing press enough to raise the consumer price index for all urban consumers (CPI-U) to 3.9 percent for the year (as of the end of September), the consumer price, index for urban wage earners and clerical workers (CPI-W) to 4.4 percent for the year, and the producer price index (PPI) to 6.9 percent for the year.

As statistician John Williams (shadowstats.com) has shown, the official inflation measures are rigged in order to hold down cost of living adjustments to Social Security recipients, thus saving money for Washington's wars. When measured correctly, the current rate of inflation in the US is 11.5 percent.

What interest rate can savers get without taking massive risks on Greek bonds? US banks pay less than one-half of one percent on FDIC insured savings deposits. Short-term US government bond funds pay essentially zero.

Thus, according to official US government statistics American savers are losing between 3.9 percent and 4.4 percent of their capital yearly. According to John Williams' estimate of the real rate of inflation, US savers are losing 22.5 percent of their accumulated savings.

As retired Americans receive no interest on their savings, they have to spend down their capital. The ability of even the most prudent retirees to survive the negative rate of interest they are receiving and the erosion by inflation of any pension that they receive will come to an end once their accumulated assets are exhausted.

Except for Washington's favored mega-rich, the one percent that has captured all of the income gains of recent years, the rest of |America has been assigned to the trash can. Nothing whatsoever has been done for them since the financial crisis, hit in December, 2007. Bush and Obama, Republican and Democrat, have focused on saving the 1 percent while giving the finger to the 99 percent.

Finally, some Americans, though not enough, have caught on to the flag-waving rah-rah "patriotism" that has consigned them to the trash bin of history. They are not going down without a fight and are in the streets. Occupy Wall Street has spread. What will be the fate of this movement?

Will the snow and ice of cold weather end the protests, or send them into public buildings? How long will the local authorities, subservient To Whom It May Concern: as they are, tolerate the obvious signal that the population lacks any confidence whatsoever in the government?

Where is the money going to come from to finance Washington's African Empire? Not from Libya's oil. Big chunks of that have been promised to the French and British for providing cover for Washington's latest way of naked aggression. Not from tax revenues from a collapsing US economy where unemployment, if measured correctly, is 23 percent.

If the protesters last, especially if they grow and don't decline, the authorities will infiltrate the protestors with police provocateurs who will fire on the police. This will be the excuse to shoot down the protestors and to arrest the survivors as "terrorists" or "domestic extremists" and to send them to the $385 million dollar camps built under US government contract by Cheney's Halliburton.

Meanwhile, lost in their oblivion, conservatives will continue to bemoan the ruination of the country by homosexual marriage, abortion, and "the liberal media". Liberal organizations committed to civil liberty will assist Washington in demonizing its next target for military attack while turning a blind eye to the war crimes of President Obama.

When we consider that Israel has got away with, being as it is under Washington's bought protection – the war crimes, the murders of children, the eviction in total disregard of international law of Palestinians from their ancestral homes, the bulldozing of their houses and uprooting of their olive groves in order to move in fanatical "settlers," the murderous invasions of Lebanon and Gaza, the wholesale slaughter of civilians – we can only conclude that , Israel's enabler, can get away with far more.

In the few opening years of the 21st century, Washington has destroyed the US Constitution, the separation of powers, international law, the accountability of government, and has sacrificed every moral principal to achieving hegemony over the world. This ambitious agenda is being attempted while simultaneously Washington removed all regulation over Wall Street, the home of massive greed, permitting Wall Street's short-term horizon to wreck the US economy, thus destroying the economic basis for Washington's assault on the world.

Will the US collapse in economic chaos before it rules the world?
COURTESY DAILY TIMES LAHORE SUNDAY OCTOBER 23, 2011.

NATO'S AGENDA FOR LIBYA:
By Vijay Prashad

'Dead men tell no tales. They cannot stand trial. They cannot name the people who helped them stay in power. All secrets die with them.'

On the dusty reaches out of Sine, a convoy flees a battlefield. A NATO aircraft fires and strikes the cars. The wounded struggle to escape, armed trucks, with armed fighters, rush to the scene. They find the injured, and among them is the most significant prize: a bloodied Muammar Qaddafi stumbles, is captured, and then is thrown amongst the fighters. One can imagine their exhilaration a cell-phone traces the events of the next few minutes. A badly injured Qaddafi is pushed around, thrown on a car, and then the video gets blurry. The next images are of a dead Qaddafi. He has a bullet hole on the side of his head.

These images go onto you tube almost instantly. They are on television, and in the newspapers. It will be impossible not to see them.

The Third Geneva Convention (article 13), "Prisoners of war must at all times be protected, particularly against acts of violence or intimidation and against insults and public curiosity".

The Fourth Geneva Convention (article 27); "Protected persons are entitled, in all circumstances, to respect for their persons, their honor, their family rights, their religious convictions and practices, and their manners and customs. They shall at all times be humanely treated, and shall be protected especially against all acts of violence or threats thereof and against insults and public curiosity."

One of the important ideological elements during the early days of the war in Libya was the framing of the arrest warrant for Qaddafi and his clique by the International Criminal Court's selectively zealous chief prosecutor Luis Moreno Ocampo. It was enough to have press reports of excessive violence for Moreno Ocampo and Ban Ki-moon to use the language of genocide; no independent, forensic evaluation of the evidence was necessary. (Actually, independent evaluation was soon forthcoming from Amnesty International and Human Rights Watch, decisively debunking Ocampo's charges. AC/JSC)

NATO sanctimoniously said that it would help the ICC prosecute the warrant (this despite the fact that the United States, NATO's powerhouse, is not a member of the ICC). This remark was echoed by the National Transitional Council, NATO's political instrument in Benghazi.

Humanitarian intervention was justified on the basis of potential or alleged violations of the Geneva Conventions. The intervention's finale is a violation of those very Conventions.

It would have been inconvenient to see Qaddafi in open court. He had long abandoned his revolutionary heritage (1969-1988), and had given himself over to the US-led War on Terror at least since 2003 (but in a fact since the late 1990s). Qaddafi's prisons had been an important fortune centre in the archipelago of black sites utilized by the CIA, European intelligence and the Egyptian security state. What stories Qaddafi might have told if he was allowed to speak in open court? What stories Saddam Hussein might have told had he too been allowed to speak in an open court? As it happens, Hussein at least entered a courtroom, even as it was more kangaroo than judicial.

No such courtroom for Qaddafi. As Naeem Mohaliemen put it, "Dead men tell no tales. They cannot stand trial. They cannot name the people who helped them stay in power. All secrets die with them."

Qaddafi is dead. As the euphoria dies down, it might be important to recall that we are dealing with at least two Qaddafi's. The first Qaddafi overthrew a lazy and corrupt monarchy in 1969, and proceeded to transform Libya along a fairly straightforward national development path. There were idiosyncrasies, such as Qaddafi's ideas about democracy that never really produced institutions of any value. Qaddafi had the unique ability to centralize power in the name of de-centralization. Nevertheless, in the national liberation Qaddafi certainly turned over large sections of the national surplus to improve the well-being of the Libyan people. It is because of two decades of such policies that the Libyan people entered the 21st century with high human development indicators. Oil helped, but there are oil nations (such as Nigeria) where the people languish in terms of their access to social goods and to social development.

By 1988, the first Qaddafi morphed into the second Qaddafi, who set aside his anti-imperialism for collaboration with imperialism, and who dismissed the national development path for neo-liberal privatization (I tell this story in Arab Spring, Libya Winter, which will be published by AK Press in the Spring of 2012). This second Qaddafi squandered the pursuit of well-being, and so took away the one aspect of his governance that the people supported. From the 1990s onward, Qaddafi's regime offered the masses the illusion of social wealth and the illusion of democracy. They wanted more, and that is the reason for the long process of unrest that begins in the early 1990s (alongside the Algerian Civil War), comes to a head in 1995-96 and then again in 2006. It has been a long slog for the various rebellious elements to find themselves.

The new leadership of "Tripoli was incubated inside the Qaddafi regime. His son, Saif al-Islam was the chief neo-liberal reformer, and he surrounded himself with people who wanted to turn Libya into a larger Dubai. They went to work around 2006, but were disillusioned by the rate of progress, and many (including Mahmud Jibril, the current Prime Minister) had threatened to resign on several occasions. When an insurgency began in Benghazi, this clique hastened to join them, and by March had taken hold of the leadership of the rebellion. It remains in their hands.

What is being celebrated on the streets of Benghazi, Tripoli and the other cities? Certainly there is jubilation at the removal from power of the Qaddafi of 1988-2011. It is in the interests of NATO and Jibril's clique to ensure that in this auto-da-fe the national liberation anti-imperialist of 1969-1988 is liquidated, and that the neo-liberal era is forgotten, to be reborn anew as if not tried before. That is going to be the trick: to navigate between the joy of large sections of the population who want to have a say in their society (which Qaddafi blocked, and Jibril would like to canalize) and a small section that wants to pursue the neoliberal agenda (which Qaddafi tried to facilitate but could not do so over the objections of his "men of the tent"). The new Libya will be born in the gap between the two interpretations.

The manner of Qaddafi's death is a synecdoche for the entire war. NATO's bombs stopped the convoy, and without them Qaddafi would probably have fled to his next reboot. The rebellion might have succeeded without NATO. But with NATO, certain political options had to be foreclosed; NATO's member states are in line now to claim their reward. However, they are too polite in a liberal European way to actually state their claim publically in a quid-pro-quo fashion. Hence, they say things like: this is a Libyan war, and that Libya must decide what it must do. This is properly the space into which those sections in the new Libyan power structure that still value sovereignty must assert themselves. The window for that assertion is going to close soon, as the deals get inked that lock Libya's resources and autonomy into the agenda of the NATO states. COURTESY DAILY TIMES LAHORE SUNDAY OCTOBER 23, 2011

MISREPRESENTATION SUBJUGATION OF GOVERNMENT BY INDIRECT PARTIES DOMESTIC

The indirect parties include all those who indirectly or directly influence the law making processes, government decision-making processes, for their own benefit or for the benefit of others, other than voters, who pay them to exert influence and get the job done for their own gains. These indirect domestic parties like media, lobbyists, businesses, corporations, NGOs', etc. Most of these indirect parties contribute financially directly or indirectly to the political parties, contesting elections in a country. All these indirect domestic parties do not generally work for the benefit of the country's public, but work for their own interests. Most of these interest groups hire/employ lobbyists for exerting influence on law makers to get their job done, to further their cause, to bring up their issues/high light their issues, to get their choice of projects/contracts, to get their choice of bills/laws passed with the intention to benefit themselves from the public kitty at the expense of country's general public. Thus the issues are resolved, the laws are made, the bills are passed to benefit these indirect domestic parties most of whom have financially supported the legislators/political parties in their hour of need (you scratch my back I will scratch yours). In addition to the financial help provided to the legislators/political parties; the relatives and close associates of legislators are employed at positions that they are not competent for, if fair employment practices are adopted.

The legislators breed corruption and feed on this corruption when gaining pecuniary benefits against affording favors to indirect domestic parties. These indirect domestic parties do not grant the same pecuniary benefits to the general public since the same has no authority to return the favor. Thus, the legislators play havoc with the country's public and their interests, as against their oath of office, and turn up to be criminals hiding their true faces under the legislative mask from the public and voters, election after election.

The lobbyists are friends of the public representatives, administration, and media representative. The lobbyists are mostly election losers, holders of public office in the past, friends of chief executives of the big corporations who have or will take advantage from their connections developed, while in the past being employed at a place of authority. Everything done by these lobbyists is in total distrust of the general public as the public interest in most of the cases is not involved or looked after by any of the parties. Thus, the oaths of office taken by the democratically elected public representatives, to serve the public in sacred trust, are grossly violated. Now in the last decade and a half of artificially inflated economies of the developed countries, "FEAR FACTOR", has been used as a tool to extract money from the public kitty, in the shape of financial help to big banks, corporations, and industries on the pretext and fear of mass unemployment leading to protests and demonstrations on the one hand and showing their importance on the other hand in providing employment to so many people and thus paying taxes into the public kitty as against increased tax burden to the public and emptying the public till by the acquisition of aid/grants from the government on the pretext of saving jobs. Whereas, the same money is used by the top brass managements to get hefty salaries and even bonuses during these difficult time, instead of taking salary cuts.

Then there is NATO taking its toll on weak countries to enforce their agenda like in Libya. Then there are commonwealth countries influencing the agenda and policies of member countries.

Open and implied threats are used in the name of humanity, democracy, freedom, helping the oppressed, removing the elected governments by instigating military action against the civilian elected government and so on by these powerful countries, international organizations, mafia, and the others, called indirect international parties forcing their agenda and policies on the weak countries, no matter how harmful these may be for the target countries which unnecessarily results in loss of lives and property of their citizens.

In case the threats do not yield the desired results financial benefits are offered to somehow convince the government to carry on agenda of these indirect international parties. Furthermore, if corruption fails to yield the desired results then reconciliatory approaches are also used to further the IIP agenda and policies. Thus, from threats to reconciliation all the approaches are tried on the target countries by the international indirect parties to carry on and meet their objectives in total disregard of the country's population welfare and well being, as well as, against the voter's and the democratic government's agenda and policies.

There are internationally organized groups and NGO's which work for their common international agenda while being scattered over across continents in different countries like America and Europe influencing the legislators for laws to be made for legalizing inhuman actions, laws derogatory to human nature, laws like same sex marriages which no religion on earth permits as this undesired/unnatural act stops the growth of human race and is against the interest of human race and humanity, laws to legalize abortion which is tantamount to killing the human race by the voters themselves as they have given the power and authority to the legislators to make laws.

There are industries supplying fire arms and ammunitions located in these strong and powerful countries which control their sales/delivery to the various countries of the world, according to their own choice (in the so called free world). The number of bullets used in these fire arms made by various countries arms and ammunition industries are way more than enough to kill the population of the world.

Once you make an arms and ammunition factory in a capitalistic environment, the aim is to run it at full capacity to make the most money out of this private investment by sale of the manufactured arms and ammunition. Now if the world is at peace, there is no demand for the arms and ammunition except the local defense (not offence) and law and order maintenance in the country, but that too once met do not become obsolete for years to come. Therefore, wars are started by these powerful and rich countries against the weak, as well as, instigating wars among different countries, or start a war within a country i.e. one group against the other group to sell their arms and run their factories at full capacity to make the most profit out of their investments. On the other hand, if the same factory be state owned, it could be shut down when the supplies are not needed and restarted in case of need. Wars are instigated resulting in loss of lives and destruction of property, for selling their arms and ammunition and products. Thus, the world is not left at peace by these industries situated inside the super powers and powerful countries, controlling their legislators and chief executives for forwarding and carrying on their negative agenda of killing the human beings and destroying their properties to make most money out of their (negative) investments.

"Shall a few designing men, for their own aggrandizement, and to gratify their own avarice, overset the goodly fabric we have been rearing at the expense of so much time, blood, and treasure? And shall we at last become victims of our own lust of gain?" GEORGE WASHINGTON. (Page 59-3500).

The bullets made in the world are more than enough to kill the population of the world, including the manufacturers. The intention of making money by supplying arms, to start a war at the behest of third indirect international party (super power or powerful countries) for the gains to the fourth party(arms manufacturers) never lets the target nation prosper whether it be a democratic government or dictatorship friendly to the third party, killing, their own people (who provided the revenue through their taxes) with their own money and who do not go with the agenda of the third party and to profit and please the third party so the fourth party profits from it; by employing the public kitty, putting up brother against brother, countrymen against countrymen; not for the sake of benevolence but for the sake of immense loss and suffering to your people and to remain in the driving seat with the support of third and fourth indirect parties then the driver in the seat is a traitor and not a benefactor of the nation.

As against the above totally negative policies of the powerful countries whose establishments are being run by the few watching only their own interest; the most prosperous nations are the ones who have relied on economic power, after learning the lessons, instead of relying on the military power. The economic power might look weak on the face of it, as against the military power but it supersedes the militarily powerful countries. Why? – Because it is for the cause of humanity's welfare and benevolence and not for its blood and destruction in countries like Japan, Korea, Taiwan.

"Men never moan over the opportunities lost to do good, only the opportunities to be bad" GREEK PROVERB. (Page 170-3500).

"A man profits more by the sight of an idiot than by the orations of the learned." ARABIAN PROVERB. (Page 191-3500)

MISREPRESENTATION MONEY LENDING AGENCIES SUCCOUR TO SUBJUGATION.

There are organizations like IMF World Bank, ECB and so on lending money to needy countries in their hour of crisis, be it to meet their balance of payment requirement or to carry out an infrastructure project or to carry out specific reforms or to save a country from default and so on. The help given in time of need or the help taken shows up in the shape of a borrower and lender and not as a helper and the one helped.

"Never run into debt, not if you can find anything else to run into" JOSH BILLINGS(PAGE#68-3500). (Page No.68-3500)

"Do not take payment in politeness." BALTASAR GRHCIAN (PAGE#68-3500). (Page No.68-3500)

Once a country is lent money in their hour of need it turns up as a borrower. Then the lender is in a position to dictate to the borrower Non-democratic dictatorial policies to safe guard his interests, as against, the democratic governments' agenda and policies at the time they were voted in. The political party in a democratic set-up once in power, and to remain in power, borrows the money from these organizations, which is called help in need, while they are hooked in need, without asking the public of the country being indebted, against their democratic agenda and policies given to the voters upon an election.

"Democracy becomes a government of bullies tempered by editors" RALPH WALDO EMERSON. (Page No.70-3500)

"Democracy gives every man the right to be his own oppressor" JAMES RUSSEL LOWELL. (Page No.70-3500)

Thus, the non-democratic or dictatorial policies against the public of countries (practicing democracies); by the governing political parties in order to make themselves look good against their controlling mafia/public, where the voter is not asked while the government gets the country into debt, then heavy debt, then huge debt, and then to non-manageable debt.

"Blessed are the young, for they shall inherit the national debt." HERBERT HOOVER. (Page No.68-3500)

"In the midst of life we are in debt" ETHEL W. MUMFORD. (Page No.68-3500)

Thus, succor by the international financial institutions in the beginning afterwards turns in to subjugation due to heavy lending involved to save the debt ridden country from default in order to receive their principal and interest payments, as against, providing relief by negotiating, re-scheduling, and suspension of repayments till the economy of the country gets better, takes off, or readjusts to the lower level of economic activity in the wake of structural changes. The financial institutions dictate the legislators/executive against the wishes/agenda/policies of the voters to make non-benevolent decisions like creating more unemployment, putting more debt burden on the public of the country. Thus making the lives of public miserable to the point of revolt where protests lead to huge loss of life in some cases as well as destruction of the country's assets.

In the debt ridden countries democratic values and sentiments are being over-taken by these indirect parties while enforcing structural and financial changes through the respective governments of the target countries to fulfill their agenda of recovering their loans and interest in order for the loan contributor/providers to enjoy the benefits of their capitalist system, where the capital has been mostly accumulated through the use of public funds channeled and then accumulated by the donors who have financially helped the political parties/legislators during an election. Thus, the public funds used for the benefit of the very few at the neglect of the general public which then leads the public to poverty and misery by the direct parties (legislators) accommodating indirect parties for making gains for themselves as well as returning the favors given to them during election.

Hence the indebted public of a country is being grinded between the bottom wheel of the government and the upper wheel of the lenders (who became lenders by the base country's channeled and then accumulated funds). Whether it may be a developing country or a developed country or a super power, the indebtedness phenomenon is the same, making the public of a country as debt ridden and fiscally overburdened to pay unfair, unjust, and heavy taxes due to no fault of their own. The benefits of tax receipts are far to less than the heavy payments of taxes paid by the country's public.

Thus, the financial priorities (to save the capitalist system and capitalists from the victimization of capitalism) dictate the policies of the indebted governments as against their consideration of democratic priorities in decision-making and as against their basic essence of democratic values which are being sacrificed in meeting financial priorities and policies. These sacrifices are made by the general public of the concerned countries due to no fault of their own. (BUT TO CAST THEIR VOTE)

"The instrument and symbol of a freeman's power to make a fool of himself and a wreck of his country" AMBROSE BIERCE (Page No.262-3500)

Considering the present situation, there is no guarantee for the future of indebted countries; that increasing the debt will land them in a better position than where they stand today (2011-2012), however, in case of default the sacrifices will certainly bring the real adjustments and a better future for the public of the country as against the few capitalists losing their capital.

Therefore, the default though will have a temporary setback. The future will be in the shape of progress with minimum taxation in the absence of debt which is source of ever increasing fiscal burden, no fear of future loss of employment, no swords of ever increasing taxes hanging over the public's head, as the heavy taxes are lowered people will have more disposable income leading to an increase in personal spending.

The democratically elected candidates and their formed governments start misrepresenting the electoral public, which has voted them in, by following the instructions of lending agencies, against the voter's choice for political party's election agenda/policies. Thus the agenda of indirect parties is carried out by the legislators for their own benefit instead of the benefit to public at large and especially the voting public.

The lending agencies/organizations/rating agencies also play havoc with the lives of general public of the concerned countries like Greece, Portugal, Ireland as well as the underdeveloped and less developed countries like Pakistan and so on, demanding undemocratic austerity measures from parliaments/executive of these countries against their sovereign status/essence for the well being of IMF/ECB and so on; and not for the well being of voting public specifically and the general public at large of these countries which otherwise are threatened with dire consequences if the financial discipline (the discipline which is against all humanitarian considerations) as designed by these organizations/agencies is not maintained to save the capitalism, that is playing havoc with the lives of ordinary citizens of these countries. The double edge sword falls on debt ridden countries, whether be it, increase in taxes met with reduction in demand and curtailment in public spending also resulting in reduced demand and employment. Thus unless economic downturn subsides and economic growth swings in the lending agencies dealing with these governments who have made their citizens laden with huge debt, without their choice, the repayments of which in future go for ages God knows how long. This cruel act on the part of lending agencies/organizations, as well as, the elected governments is playing havoc with their democratic agenda and policies for which they have not been voted in. Thus the democratic essence of these countries is being marred by the dictatorial norms of lending agencies/organizations and rating agencies.

Late 2011, the IMF/EU Auditors are forcing the Greek government to carry out non democratic reforms in the country's transport system and justice system in order to privatize a part of public transport system and form a speedy justice system for the release of another installment of debt (aid).

The overburdened and debt ridden countries governments are so worrisome for the sake of organization of the affluent (made affluent by the democratic system of governments) i.e. ECB-IMF-WB-OCD and G-20 countries that the chief executive of these organizations providing loan to the countries entangled in their net are having a meeting in Berlin late 2011 on the threats to their global financial system as well as **"risks to the global economy that have been laid bare in the financial crisis", as stated by George Stieter.**

FEUDAL LORDS/EXTORTIONISTS/NAWABS/ VAGABONDS:

The feudal lords/nawabs/extortionists/vagabonds elected as legislators in developing countries bring social inequality and injustice to the voters and general public which is against all the religions. These privileged ones get their vested interests fulfilled in education / employment / beauru-cracy / foreignecracy / justice / policing and so on. Pakistan is still stuck with the feudal lords / nawabs and so on who treat themselves as rulers forcing the poor to get their votes whether they like them or not and consider their voters to be their personal servants who put them in parliament which in turn rob the poor / weak in every available manner through corruption/extortion and so on while enjoying full immunity from any policing/justice system as part of or even not part of the government and these are worst of the worst mostly in countries of Indian sub-continent, Africa, South East Asia, etc. These are the rulers ruling, and not the democratically elected candidates serving the people as they have to, against the oath of office taken by them.

These rulers with feudal mentality are the landlords / businessmen elite industrialists elite/vagabonds/extortions and so on having mostly interwoven family networks found at the helm of each political party whether be it a governing party or opposition party making a fun of the voting public who in most cases are their faithful dogs and not human beings thus letting these politicians carry on their aristocratic style in these modern time.

Now when the poor do not get avowed representation how will the policy makers understand the need of these masses deprived of humanely needs and facilities as well as privileges. The situation might be worse in some other countries like Somalia, Thailand and so on to name one each in Africa and East Asia, however, in Pakistan – the Indian sub-continent the situation is so bad that all these politicians are brothers among themselves who get their votes and never discuss the plight of their voters in the so called autocratic parliament bracing a friendly environment. There has not been any serious debate in

Pakistan at least since 2008 thus they all have plundered the wealth of the poor and have brought the country to a break up point.

Reference: **Dawn Monday May 17, 2010.**

CHAPTER SIX

POLITICAL PARTIES – LEADERS – CANDIDATES, TRAITORS OR PATRIOTS

POLITICAL PARTIES – LEADERS – CANDIDATE TRAITORS OR PATRIOTS:

Political parties are formed on the basis of common ideologies, interests and objectives (social, economic, religions, etc.), whereas, the leaders who are opportunists/reformers/originators, emerge to get the control of the country's government for securing a position of authority for themselves and to further their personal agenda/party agenda and not the public's agenda. The number of political parties in a country each carry their own and different agenda and policies presented to the public for its selection by the eligible voters on the election day or during election period and from among the eligible voters only the voters who exercise their right to vote are counted for the success or failure of the candidate contesting election.

It is hard to find a leader who is patriotic, work's for the benefit of the country, works for the benefit of his country's population, looks after the interests of his country above all the other interests of his political party, his financial supporters, his own group of people i.e. close associates, relatives, strong supporters, flatterers, hypocrites, and so on who encircle him/her to get their own benefits at the expense of public at large as long as he/she stays in power/authority in total disregard of voters choice/public's rights.

The leadership of political parties can be broadly categorized as under:-

(i) The leadership of a political party is in the hand of a family or family run political party,

(ii) The leadership of a political party is in the hands of a democratically elected leader; elected by the party members and not the country's population.

(ii) The leadership of a political party forced upon the party members through dictatorial norms/self made heirs of the leadership upon the death/deposition/retirement of the leader.

The No. 1 and 3 have the most common attributes with the only big difference that the leader in No. 3 after taking over the party by hook or crook starts working and affording benefits to the close associates so as they take strong side of him/her in converting the party leadership to family leadership leading to autocracy and then to kingship. Thus, political parties formed on family basis (No.1) or taken over by an individual as in (No. 3) generally try to make it, a family run party having no public or party consensus. The party affiliates generally having bad conduct cling to the party leadership like slaves in order to gain the benefits for themselves as long as the party holds to power. The party affiliates have no common ideology/consensus as they only support their leadership policies to please their leader irrespective of the benefits, if any, delivered to the public and country at large, and follow the leader blindly to gain maximum benefits for themselves while in power. In most cases, the leader leads the country against the welfare of general public to make him/her an essential commodity, without whom as leader, the country would not survive. But in fact he/she is cheating the public of his country at large while resorting to carry out his/her own personal agenda of acquiring and building his/her personal factories, amassing funds through corruption, commissions on the award of big projects to contractors, buying, importing and leasing of different items from abroad for different state run companies, amassing money through extortion from the business community, resorting to white collar crime with the help of government run organizations controlled by their close affiliates who have been appointed through unfair and corrupt means, receiving commissions from contractors who have been awarded contracts out of the way by them, channeling public funds through third and fourth parties for their misappropriations. To sum it up the political parties taken over by the so called corrupt, illiterate, inexperienced and the one's having bad and deplorable conduct as they are tax cheaters, extortionists, embezzlers and so on and, above all, the traitors of their country, plundering and shifting the bread and butter of the masses to their foreign bank accounts. Some of these leaders are permanent residents of other countries who while residing abroad lead a political party at their home country which subsists on extortion.

Most of the autocratic rulers ruling for decades (Libya, Tunisia, Egypt) under the disguise of democracy by holding elections which were always farce. These autocratic rulers turned tyrant, have not been able, to establish themselves as servants of the masses but remained cruel and corrupt dictators plundering the wealth of their countrymen and amassing the same in foreign banks. Sir Ivan Jennings has described it in his book party politics III the stuff of politics, "It is also a matter of class-interest, because those who are doing well out of a particular situation think it excellent and wish to preserve it, while the underdogs are satisfied that it needs radical reforms" (P.15 The two party system). These tyrant rulers have practiced dictatorship under the disguise of democracy in one form or the other with the help of their captive legislators making legislations as desired by their masters to hold a solid grip on the country's administration, thus term after term farce elections were held to justify the ill fated democracy. These tyrant rulers always had a tiny population of greedy and selfish human beings turned dogs by wagging their tails while putting their heads down against the masters. Thus the so called system of governance failed to protect and serve the interests of the ordinary citizens in total disregard of their political and economic preferences.

On the other hand, political parties formed on the basis of common ideologies whether social, economic, religious etc., and the leader of the party elected through a democratic process to lead the party normally heads the country/province or state government whatever the case may be (NOT IN INDIA where the party leader is Sonia Gandhi and Prime Minister is Man Mohan Singh) with some exceptions when the party wins avowed representation in an election. However, a much different position emerges when the party leadership instead of heading the country upon receiving a mandate through election nominates the most suitable (educated – experienced – tolerant – gentleman – one who has good conduct, etc.) person to lead the country (like India) to further the interest of the voters, country, and party instead of the party leadership taking control of the country whether he/she is qualified or not to lead the country and the party. Thus in the later case the interest of the country, voters, and general public takes preference over the party leader's self interest.

The political parties organized, managed and run under a democratically elected leadership/office bearers normally have low self interests as against; the family run parties; and the parties with a leader imposed upon the party by hook and crook, or by default, or by death of the leader and so on. Generally in the family run parties the leadership neither leave's the party nor the government once elected to form a government thus their self interests are way higher than the democratically elected leadership/office bearers. The leader's self interests naturally puts the voters, general public, and country interests behind their personal interests of gaining authority not to serve the voters, public, and country but to plunder the wealth of the country to get rich richer and richest. The same situation develops for the party leadership taken over by hook or crook, or by default, or by death of the leader and so on, the self interests of the party leadership takes precedence over the interests of the voters, public and country.

The cause of leadership to falter and fail is rooted in undemocratic party structures, tribal culture, feudal culture, selection of candidates in an election not on the basis of their conduct, education, and experience but one who can grab votes by hook or crook through the tribal/baradari/feudalism or through village area headman; in total disregard of his/her character and conduct, as he/she may be a convict/extortionist/corrupt mafia leader/or a famous character famous for his/her evil deeds. Thus the whimsy leader emerges as lawmaker as against leadership cherishing democratic values like following the agenda/policies he/she got elected, law abiding, showing good conduct and planning for the better future of his constituents/countrymen.

The whimsy candidates follow the whims of their leader without properly evaluating any of his actions whether good or bad for the country and its masses. Thus nodding yes; to every good and bad action of their leader in flattery which in turn; turns to sycophant. Thus the, worthless, traitor, corrupt, extortionist, characterless, and one with worst conduct is considered to be sacred and one who questions his actions turns to be sacrilegious committing sacrilege, Alas! When the public comes out on the streets and the sacred autocrat turned tyrant reaches his end result the sacredness turns to treason as the same unpatriotic leader has stolen the wealth of the country through corruption/extortion and so on; and has hidden this wealth in foreign countries and their banks so the thief and his/her associates can have a luxurious life for ages to come at the cost of his/her beloved people of the country who bore with him/her for his/her selfish gains against their own loss and bleak future. The wealth thus shifted abroad in most cases stays abroad, according to the good or bad intentions of the country holding that wealth and providing refuge to the plunderer;

for and against, the country, and the people whose, wealth has been plundered. In some cases, this plundered wealth has been returned back to the country from where it was plundered for the sake of the people of that country as a goodwill gesture. In most cases, if the follow up is good and forceful as well as retaliatory the beloved leader and sacred cow turned traitor meets his/her end not alone but also along with his family for which he/she amassed wealth through corruption, extortion, etc. and committed treason.

Thus, the democratic system to function effectively the political parties of a country should practice and operate strictly within the democratic values for choosing their leadership and office bearers, as against, family basis parties and default leadership parties by imposing a leader on the party as against proposing a leader for the party. It has been observed that the successful leaders and their political parties have broad based agenda i.e., accommodating majority population of the country for their welfare and well-being, as against narrow agenda of watching for the welfare of one community like business community or labor community or agriculture community, and ignoring the others. The chosen agenda and policies of the party along with their chosen leader, who if in a position to form the government will carry out the agenda and policies stated at the time of election for which the mandate is given by the voters who exercised their right to vote, thus actions should follow the words in complete harmony.

A viable democratic system established through democratically run political party and thus their chosen leader and then elected leader; from his/her constituency! ONLY; is a crucial factor for the sustenance of a viable democracy in countries practicing democratic system of government.

SAME CANDIDATE – SAME VOTERS – DIFFERENT PARTIES
GOOD VERSUS BAD CONDUCT

Generally there are two types of candidates contesting elections on the platform of different parties in different elections, one; who is liked by the constituency voters for his/her good conduct in the past, worked for the betterment of the constituents, always stood for the right against the wrong, made good on his/her promises with the constituents, stood up to fight against the agenda/policies of his/her party harmful for the constituents and the country. Who equally treated all his/her constituents of different colors, creeds, religions; so on so forth. Two who is disliked by the constituents voters for his bad conduct, worked for his selfish gains as against the betterment of the constituents, always stood with the wrong against the right and turned away from the promises made with the constituents on the pretext of following the party leadership and policies even if these are against the constituents and the country, discriminating against the constituents on the basis of association, color, creed, religion as well as breeding corruption.

After all these misgivings which are generally not brought to the notice of the voters regarding the candidate having bad conduct, thus these cheaters successfully cheat the public time and time again. Now let us examine the public that gets cheated election after election especially in developed countries. Generally, election after election the same professional politicians are the only available candidates in their constituencies to the voters; some of these stick to their parties through thick and thin while the others keep on switching political parties and go with the most favorite expected to win in the coming election; in order for themselves to stay in an avowed representation election after election. In the developing countries voters have a very high illiteracy rate and thus are unable to evaluate as to the practicability of the given agenda/policies of the political parties taking part in an election. In most cases the promised agenda/policies, cannot be practically fulfilled in real life as these are highly boasted and inflated lies to get vote

The political parties generally nominate their candidates for different ridings considering the success rate to form a government irrespective of the conduct and character of the candidates, which in majority of less developed countries is deplorable.

There are different situations arising between the political parties and their nominated candidates in order to maximize the chances of the party to get the most seats in a legislature.

SITUATION – 1: When a political party leadership has a strong standing in an election race, and the votes will be cast on the basis of making that political party succeed in an election, then the party is in a position to select and put forward candidates having good education, character and conduct; of course! Only the rich ones are selected who could bear the election expenses.

SITUATION – 2: When a political party has an average standing in an election, then the party is not in a position to select and put forward the best candidates but to stay with the old lot irrespective of their conduct and character; of course! These are the ones who have experience of bearing the election expenses and recovering many fold of their election expenses after being elected.

SITUATION – 3: When a political party has a weak standing in an election, the party is left with no choice but to get the leftovers, able to bear their election expenses, irrespective of their education, character and conduct.

SITUATION – 4: When a political candidate has a good repute and a strong standing in the constituency who can get elected with any political party or else can also succeed as an independent in an election, be rich and bear election expenses.

SITUATION – 5: When a candidate has an average standing in the constituency and cannot succeed without the help of a political party of course be rich and could bear the election expenses.

SITUATION – 6: Where a candidate has a weak standing and cannot succeed without the help of a political party having strong standing in an election of course he/she should be rich to bear the expenses.

The high illiteracy rate in the less developed countries along with traditional support system through family heads, casts, village headman, etc., which is normally in total disregard of the common sense and logical reasoning for the selection of a candidate and political party, results in, the support of a candidate having a bad character and conduct thus the legislature basket gets filled with bad apples supporting each other irrespective of the visible bad marks on the skin due to various diseases and germs growing inside the apples, like corruption, fraud, extortion and so on.

On the other hand, the voters with a low illiteracy rate can to some extent evaluate the policies and agenda of the political parties and the character and conduct of the candidates, however, the choice is limited among the candidates contesting an election and the voters are choice less in choosing and nominating a candidate of their choice due to the present political party set up system where you cannot select but elect the selected one of democratic euphoria.

Furthermore the conduct of the general public if generally bad and mostly is in less developed countries the voters switch their choices on the basis of extortion and corruption i.e., to vote for the candidate who pays the most to the voters to get their votes, thus the characterless and bad conduct public puts forward a characterless candidate who breed corruption and extortion and the same characterless and bad conduct public then rests the blame on the candidate elected by their voters and votes. Thus, the majority of criminals enter the legislature – so! What do you expect? Naturally the corrupt voters from among the majority of corrupt public leads to the corrupt and criminal legislators denying justice to the few from amongst the majority, who are honest, have good character and conduct among people of a country.

"In politics stupidity is not a handicap." (Page No.183-3500)

"In politics the choice is constantly between two evils." JOHN MORLEY. (Page No.183-3500)

"Too bad ninety percent of the politicians give the other ten percent a bad reputation." HENRY KISSINGER. (Page No.183-3500)

"Any man with a fine shock of hair, a good set of teeth, and a bewitching smile can park his brains, if he has any, and run for public office." FRANK DANE. (Page No.183-3500)

CANDIDATE – REPRESENTING VOTERS OR POLITICAL PARTY:

The voters vote for the candidate or a political party or both depending upon the strong standing either one or both enjoy in an election. Generally, the voters who know the candidate very well due to his/her past performance honesty, truthfulness, and just representation of their cause, vote for the candidate in an election to place him/her in the avowed representation as a candidate with good conduct from their constituency.

On the other hand the constituents who are not within the close proximity of the candidate and do not know him/her in person or through association from others, the voters rely on the party that he/she represents and thus vote for the party of their choice and not the candidate of their choice.

Most of the time political parties have dual agenda i.e., one that is publicized and the other one that is hidden. The voters are aware of the publicized agenda and not aware of the hidden agenda.

Normally in a fair election a candidate displaying good conduct in the past, for which he/she is known in the public might win the election despite the deplorable results of his/her party in an election on the other hand a not very well known or established candidate of a political party might lose the election besides his/her good character and conduct even when his/her party shows excellent performance in an election. Thus, personal contact with the voters and publicity plays a very important role for the candidate to win in an election besides the strong standing of his/her party in an election.

With the exception of the above, the voters generally select the candidate on the basis of political leadership of the party along with the given agenda/policies of the political party and the candidate takes a second place. This is the point where the bad apple enter the political process/arena and get inducted due to the popularity of political leadership as against their own education, experience, ability, character and conduct. In this case the voting public votes for the party on the basis of their experience and trust on the leadership of the party as well as delivery of their agenda/policies once the party forms the government and the unknown candidate gets elected even when not publicized.

The candidate of a political party generally stands with his party leadership as against the interest of the voters who have put him/her in avowed representation when the party leadership works against the interest and wishes of the voters. Thus, generally the candidate forwards the cause of the party as against forwarding the cause of the constituents, therefore, misrepresenting the voters after gaining their trust for their fair and just representation. Now the candidate once elected on a party platform is part of the political party, and not the voters who have voted him/her in and thus are left with no recourse to kick the representative out before next election which is due after four or five years. During the election campaign which is normally very short lived the candidate has most interaction with the constituents, whereas, the party leader touring the various constituencies in support of his/her candidates forwards the agenda/policies of the party for the next four to five years before the voters of the country.

On the other hand, the contesting candidate interacting with voters for most of the time reverses his/her position after being elected and starts interacting with his party leadership and office holders, and generally never ever reverts back to the voters for their input and, comments, to alleviate their sufferings, to solve their problems and so on as against justifying the policies of his party whether beneficial for the public or not. He/she thrusts their party's view point on the public and constituents instead of thrusting the voters viewpoints upon the party leadership; so much so; that the party's policies start supporting the policies of the mafia who once supported the party financially during the election campaign, as well as mafia outside the country – big powers who constantly threaten the government with dire consequences if their policies are not imposed against the interests of country's majority. The voters in control only on Election Day, once cast their votes cut their hands from the ruling majority party who can either harm them or make them prosper (generally follow the third and fourth party agenda forced upon them against the party agenda).

"I always voted at my party's call, AND never thought of thinking for myself at all. I thought so little, they rewarded me by

making me the Ruler of the Queens Navel" W.S.GILBERT. (Page No.183-3500)

"An honest politician is one who when he is bought stays bought" SIMON CAMERON. (Page No.182-3500)

"The two maxims of any great man at court are, always to keep his countenance and never to keep his word." JONATHAN SWIFT. (Page No.184-3500)

In politics "you can fool too many people too much of the time" JAMES THURBER. (Page No.184-3500)

"There are hardly two creatures of a more differing species than the same, when pretending to a place and when in possession of it." SIR GEORGE SAVILE. (Page No.185-3500)

CHAPTER SEVEN

FINANCIAL BURDEN OF DEMOCRACY ON A NATION

FINANCIAL BURDEN OF DEMOCRACY ON A NATION

Democratic governments put immense financial burden on the public of their countries by maintaining election ministries, institutions, electoral rolls, carrying out election after the completion of electoral term which normally runs for four to five years or before that in case of no confidence vote leading to fall of the government, or due to the death/resignation of an elected representative.

Thus, the immense financial burden of an election is more than complemented by the ever-increasing expenses of the elected members in the shape of salaries, election grants, traveling expenses, office maintenance expenses, expenses on foreign visits and so on. The above list excludes the immense expenses incurred by the political parties and their candidates for election campaigns, be it, presidential election or congressional election, general election, senate election and so on.

The fact that immense spending takes place in an election campaign is evident by the statement, "In 1987-88 election cycle, political candidates and committees at all levels – federal, state and local – spent $ 2.7 billion on political campaigns" (Financing the 1988 elections). If we make a fair estimate of rising prices and the services used of the ever-increasing number of different media channels, newspapers, etc. the election spending double's from the previous election to the next election. There is not much literature available for the financial impact on public treasury of maintaining democratic system of governments in various developed and less developed countries. It is estimated that in 2014 Indian election campaign spending amounted to $ 5/= billion The layer upon layers of elected politicians that is at federal, state/provincial, city/municipal levels get salaries, perks, grants, pensions, office and staff maintenance expenses and so on for representing their riding/constituency/district in a legislature, be it, parliament, congress, senate, provincial assembly, state legislature, municipal hall/city hall, leads one to think whether the public is facilitated by their presence in alleviating the financial burden in the shape of reduced taxes; or is over burdened with debt which comes in the shape of increase in taxes at all levels i.e., municipal, state, and federal; and a further lack of efficiency due to different layers of legislation and administrations, and the assertion is supported by, "The members of party staff have increased universally, ranging from massive 330 percent increase in Ireland (and almost the same in Germany), to the more modest increases in Britain and the Netherlands ------ it is often real or potential access to public office which has enhanced the ability of the parities to accumulate organizational resources such as staff and money." (P6&7) Peter Mair.

The absence of political jargon during the months before the run off to elections in most democratic countries, results in the governments being run smoothly and efficiently as the political interests, which further their financial interests are absent; thus politicians do create more problems while solving few in the course of making themselves as political heroes. Thus, it is evident and is a fact that the governments can and do function smoothly and more efficiently in the absence of the political entities; with far less burden on the public kitty, far less problems for the general public, far-far less media hysteria, and far less proud politicians thus leading to lower taxes and cheaper products and services otherwise not well within the reach of general public of a country. When we add up all the financial costs of maintaining a democratic system of government that too including direct costs and indirect costs in the developed as well as under-developed countries a big chunk of the concerned country's GNP is wasted for the rich as against the welfare of the poor.

The accommodation of indirect parties from the public kitty amounts to a very huge financial burden upon the general public of the countries with balanced budget/surplus budgets in the shape of higher taxes (less disposable income) and in case of deficit financing the general public of the country, paying even higher taxes, to cater for the interest payments and repayment of principal amount, thus, foregoing the opportunity of spending the same money on the welfare of the general public, and if the government bails out some of these indirect parties from the public kitty in the shape of support payments, grants, etc. then the public have to pay even higher taxes.

"The excessive increase of any thing causes a reaction in the opposite direction " (PLATO). (Page No.207-3500)

"Prosperity discovers vice, diversity discover virtue" (FARICS BACON). (Page No.193-3500)

"Virtue has never been as respectable as money " (MARK TWAIN). (Page No.261-3500)

"The principle of spending money to be paid by posterity, under the name of funding, is but swindling futurity on a large scale" Thomas Jefferson. (Page No.240-3500)

"The marvel of all history is the patience with which men and women submit to burdens unnecessarily laid upon them by their governments. "William E. Borah. (Page No.240-3500)

"Taxation without representation is tyranny." Attributed to James Otis. (Page No.239-3500)

The right to tax someone gives the tax payer the right to claim the benefits of its disbursement.

Let us compare and examine annual salaries of the head of states of few democratically run governments of the world excluding the vast majority of layers over layers of federal, provincial, and municipal members

Singapore Prime Minister	=	Sg$2.2 million (US $1.69 million (after 36% reduction).
President of the USA	=	US$ 400,000
Prime Minister of India	=	US$ 36,200
Singapore President	=	Sg$ 1.54 million (after 50% (ceremonial) (Reduction)
Singapore Entry Leve	=	Sg$ 1.1 million Cabinet Minister
German Chancellor	=	Euro 230,000
Hong Kong Chief Executive	=	$ 543,500
Prime Minister of Japan	=	$ 513,000

The above stated facts corroborate our findings of huge burden of democracy on the people of a country, besides the extra huge burden of an election and an election campaign.

The number of legislature seats in various countries where the salaries, perks, and pensions are paid from the public kitty, to mention a few; Australia (150), Canada (308), France (577), India (543), UK (646), USA House (435), Germany (598), Hungary (386), Italy (630), Japan (480), New Zealand (12), Russia (450), Israel (12), Saudi Arabia (400), Spain (350), Austria (183), Belgium (150), Chile (12), Denmark (175), Finland (199), Netherlands (150), Ireland (166). (Source: The Politics of Electoral Systems P616).

CHAPTER EIGHT

OATH OF OFFICE

OATH OF OFFICE

An oath of office from an appointed / elected / selected / inherited / default appointment and so on office holder is a requirement that an oath taker is obligated to fulfill as stated in the office holders oath of office. Thus, the oath taker as obligated by oath should never ever run into oblivion. An oblivious oath taker, if not honest, leads with his oath to treason, denies justice to the subjects, facilitates corruption, looses trust, and so on, the list goes on and on, perfidy turns to perjury. Perjury leads the rapacious office holders to deny justice to the subjects; leading the country, community and society to abyss.

The oath establishes a trust relationship in the Omni-presence of God (by holding his/her book, swearing by his/her name, and so on) between the oath taker and the subjects, whose rights, interests, etc. are being protected and watched by the oath taker in the case of people of the book i.e., Jews, Christians, and Muslims. The other religions do as well take oath according to their theological values.

The oath is administered by a figure under oath traditionally recognized in the constitution/tradition and normally one step above the oath taker or else by a judge of the respective courts as provided by the constitution. There are different practices in different countries of oath administration mostly by swearing in while putting their hands on the holy book or while holding their respective holy book in their right hand. The practice of administering oath of office by laying hands on the holy book or holding the book is naturally more authentic than taking an oath of office without the book. The oath by the book naturally provides more strength to a person of good conduct, to do justice to all the subjects, whereas the oath without the book provides opportunity to a person having bad conduct to avoid and escape the wrath of Almighty the Omnipotent, the Omni present, and the Omniscient for dissimulating as he/she did not touch the book and thus oath is not binding on him/her as against; taking the oath by laying hands or holding the holy book in his/her right hand.

Generally the oath of office for public servants and political appointees owe allegiance to protect and preserve the constitution of a country whether written or evolved traditionally and owe allegiance to the country as well as do justice between and to all. The violation of oaths of office provides grievous penalties ranging from dismissal of the office holder to his/her death generally around the world but the same are taken for granted in countries full of corruption, people with bad conduct not practicing true religious values.

"**The best liar is he who makes the smallest amount of lying goes the longest way** "SAMUEL BUTLER. (Page No.143-3500)

"**In lapidary inscription a man is not upon oath**" SAMUEL JOHNSON. (Page No.167-3500)

"**When a man assumes a public trust he should consider himself a public property**" THOMAS JEFFERSON. (Page No.183-3500)

Two samples of oath from the constitution of Pakistan are given below along with discussion to explain the points related to oaths and oath taking in an Islamic country.

President (Article 42)

(In the name of Allah, The most Beneficent, The most Merciful.)

I,_____, do solemnly swear that I am a Muslim and believe in the Unity and Oneness of almighty Allah, the Books of Allah, the Holy Quran being the last of them, the Prophet hood of Muhammad (peace be upon him) as the last of the Prophets and that there can be no Prophet after him, the Day of Judgment, and all the requirements and teachings of the Holy Quran and Sunnah:

That I will bear true faith and allegiance to Pakistan:

That, as President of Pakistan, I will discharge my duties, and perform my functions, honestly, to the best of my ability, faithfully in accordance with the Constitution of the Islamic Republic of Pakistan and the law, and always in the interest of the sovereignty, integrity, solidarity, well-being and prosperity of Pakistan.

That I will not allow my personal interest to influence my official conduct or my official decisions:

That I will preserve, protect and defend the Constitution of the Islamic Republic of Pakistan:

That, in all circumstances, I will do right to all manner of people, according to law, without fear or favor, affection or ill-will:

And that I will not directly or indirectly communicate or reveal to any person any matter which shall be brought under my consideration or shall become known to me as President of Pakistan, except as may be required for the due discharge of my duties as President.

May Allah Almighty help and guide me (Amen).

In the above given oath of office for the president of Pakistan. The oath taker solemnly swears that he/ she is a muslim. Therefore, One; he/she should not be elected if he was not a muslim. Two; if he/she is a muslim then there is no need for him/her to say that he/ she believes in unity and oneness of Allah, the holy Quran , the prophet-hood of MUHAMMAD (peace be upon him)as the last prophet. Three; and if he/she believes on the day of judgment and the requirements and teachings of holy Quran and sunnah then the next three paragraphs in the oath are not necessary under the oath for oath taker. Four; There is not a single oath taker since to date who has preserved, protected, and defended the constitution of Islamic Republic of Pakistan because the rights of the citizens of Pakistan are blatantly violated as against provided in oath to be preserved, protected, and defended under the constitution by president of Pakistan. Injustice is for the rich and corrupt, and justice for the poor and innocent. The constitution is not being preserved, protected, and defended for the masses but is laid bare for the corrupt and affluent to gain from it as it suits to them. The rich and corrupt escape justice and the poor and innocent ones are held to account for it. Basic necessities are not provided for the masses, who are treated as lower class untouchables as in Hinduism, in an Islamic country. On the other hand, if the president of Pakistan has to preserve, protect, and defend the constitution of Pakistan then what is the role of other office holders and institutions as the country stands out as one of the most corrupt in the world.

Members of the Armed Forces

(Article 244)

(In the name of Allah, the most Beneficent, the most Merciful).

I,_____, do solemnly swear that I will bear true faith and allegiance to Pakistan and uphold the Constitution of the Islamic Republic of Pakistan which embodies the will of the people, that I will not engage myself in any political activities whatsoever and that I will honestly and faithfully serve Pakistan in the Pakistan Army (or Navy or Air Force) as required by and under the law.

May Allah Almighty help and guide me (Amen).

In the above given oath of office for the members of the armed forces "uphold the constitution of Islamic Republic of Pakistan which embodies the will of the people". The country being run under the umbrella of 1973 constitution, written and passed, almost four decades ago, with 40 million registered bogus votes as revealed now, by the most honest election commission of Pakistan and innumerous ghost polling stations. Then how could the constitution embody the will of the people of Pakistan. If the masses are asked about their will today in a referendum they will surely demand the severest available punishment for the government and its allies.

Reference: Dawn Friday March 5, 2010.

CHAPTER NINE

ANOMALIES OF DEMOCRACY

ANOMALIES OF DEMOCRACY

The basic foundation of democracy is vote. The voter must be eligible and listed in order to exercise his/her right to vote. In any election, the number of total votes cast, out of the total eligible and listed voters are the voters interested in the democratic system of government, whereas, the rest remain indifferent and are not at all interested in the democratic style of government for various negative reasons, like all the candidates are considered as working for their own selfish ends and the voters do not like the democratic system of government which is not delivering the due benefits to the common citizens. The voters are not interested to vote as their vote is not going to bring any change towards the betterment of the public at large, the establishment controlling the government and legislature or the mafia cannot be separated from the government.

The democratic style of government refrains from accommodating the population of the country and instead, only accommodates the voters who voted for the party that formed the government in the past and are likely voters to vote for the same political party again, if the previously declared election agenda of the party has been met.

On the other hand, if the percentage of voters not voting in an election is greater than the percentage of voters voting that clearly leads us to conclude that the majority is not interested in democratic style of government.

You can vote the legislative members in the legislature but you cannot vote them out until the end of their term even when the ruling party does not follow the election agenda, plays havoc with the economy, sign's bad deals/contracts with domestic or foreign donors/ agencies/ companies, sign's bad treaties with other countries so on and the list goes on. In the case of strong government and weak opposition the strikes/street protests are organized to bring down the governments at the immense loss of lives and property as well as the economy of the country. World over millions of people have been killed and hundreds are being killed daily to bring down the democratic governments working against the interests of their citizens behaving like staunch dictators.

The legislature members are elected for four to five years term depending upon the declared time span of the of election and the ones, who are responsible for making bad and defective laws are never held responsible for the society's ills and misgivings that they have created. The same laws are applied to future generations sunk in debt who are not beneficiaries of debt in the debt ridden countries by the party in power to stay in the avowed representation i.e., for the benefit of the few at the expense the greater majority. Thus, the inheritance of bad laws is an evil act for the public which has never participated or associated with the legislature at all.

The laws made by the legislatures elected for a term by the present generation of voters are applied to the future generations of voters which have no links whatsoever with the legislature passing the laws being applied on them.

The laws passed by one elected legislature cannot be enforced on the public and voters of the next term as those previous legislatures were not elected by these voters.

As opposed to the segmented voters and legislatures in a country one person rule is far better where the ruler is servant of the people and not a dictator, being responsible to all the people from new born to one's close to the end of their life for any of his/her good or bad deeds, laws or decrees, and so on passed and imposed by him/her on the populations of a country. Whereas, while making or abandoning a law for the benefit of the population at large you do not have to wait for years or for the legal hustling for years to change a law if you have the right persons and right reasons to convince one person that the law is for the betterment of the population. The financial expenses of democracy when eliminated, naturally the taxes will be way lower. Thus, if there are no political parties there is no plutocracy, no voters needed to dictate the conduct of plutocrats and their associates thriving on the public money as in democratic system of governance, there is no widespread corruption, no misrepresentation of population as everybody from new born to the end of their lives is considered and accounted for, no divisions in the population of the nation, communities, and households.

Thus, the blame game which is a norm of democracy i.e., our political party inherited the deficit, the war, the recession, the unemployment and so on, that is all the negativity to be assigned to the previous government is totally eradicated as the one man/woman responsible for the government is to be blamed for any negative aspects brought out for which he/she is in control.

Thus, if your party takes over power by hook or crook, then plays havoc with the economy of the country, destroys all the public institutions/resources, destroys the business base of the country, surpasses all records of corruption where the illiterate head of the state is the most corrupt and famous for being called Mr. Ten percent by the media who plunged the country into extra ordinary huge internal and external debt; and the opposition joins hand with the government, as friendly opposition, thus the opposition is then considered worse than the government by losing their trust with the people of the country as saviors of the population and watchers of their voters interests. Thus the opposition sides with the government sharing the corruption booty with the government as against the ever increasing plight of the people by keeping quiet at the destruction of the country as they have to take over the country's next government as agreed between the two major parties at the expense of destroying the country by playing friendly opposition in Pakistan.

In the case of Caliph (there are no caliphs now), Amir, there are no Amirs now!, in the case of King all the subjects are treated equally in the kingdom as there are no political parties dividing the nation by the choice of their voters, there are no party members and party favorites (who finance the political parties), all the important decisions can be taken at once to correct any untoward situation, or to gain the benefit out of a situation for the country or nation, there are no democratic form of government maintenance expenses, taxes are way lower than the countries practicing democracies. Any matter in the interest of the country can be decided at once instead of gathering the legislature members and waiting for them to form a consensus on the issue on hand and then vote on the issue which sometime is not in the interest of legislatures thus could not be at all achieved and the benefits to accrue are thus lost for the nation.

The world's watchers of democracy like the USA and European Union whose legislators and elected heads have never been given mandate by their voters during an election for over throwing the legitimate governments of other countries whether dictatorial or democratic not siding with them. Whereas, protecting the dictators, tyrants and the farce democracies against all the norms of moral and ethical values and good conduct in the world siding with them.

Monte Palmer and William R. Thompson write, "despite the fact that governmental forms have changed considerably since Aristotle's time, his typology has always impressed people as being extremely useful – even two thousand years after its constitution. The reason for this is that Aristotle managed to tap a very basic distinction by asking two central questions about politics: who can rule, who benefits from the rule. Aristotle's answer was that the number of eligible rulers in a system would be either one, for, or many and that the rulers either ruled for the benefit of the masses or for their own benefit. This three by two division produces six types of systems. A system in which only one person was eligible to rule was classified as a KINGSHIP, if the rule benefited the masses, and a TYRANNY if it benefited only the ruler. A system in which only a few people were eligible to rule was labeled an ARISTOCRACY if it benefited the masses, and an *oligarchy* if it benefited only elite rulers. Finally, a system in which many people were eligible to rule was considered a *polity* if it benefited he masses, and a *democracy* if it benefited only the rulers, who, in this case, were assumed to be poor.

Why these particular criteria? It happens that Aristotle believed that the primary beneficiaries of political rule should be the people who are ruled. That is, political office holders should work for the common interest of all the system's members and not merely for the benefit of some smaller group."

Thus, the definition of democracy according to Aristotle assumes that the rulers are poor, therefore, democracy is a misnomer of plutocracy as the rulers are rich playing the game of rich that is rich getting ever richer. The poor can never afford to contest elections thus can never contest elections.

The elections are the pillar of plutocracy called democracy where only the rich and affluent can take part and the poor can only exercise their right to vote for the rich who will rule them.

"Politics: A strife of interest's masqueaching as a contest of principles. The conduct of public affairs for private advantage." AMBROSE BIERCE(184-3500)

"Sure now, every child knows what's government. It's half a dozen gintlemen as' the loike may be, that meets an' thinks what's best fer thimsilves, an' thin says that's best fer us – an' that's guvermint." AN ILLITERATE CIVIL WAR WIDOW(108-3500)

"Once businessmen are appointed to public office they run the government like nobody's business." (P 108 -3500)

"Democracy is a charming form of government, full of confusion and variety and dispensing a sort of equality to equals." PLATO(86-3500)

In the democratic style of government, there are no consistent policies and programs for the public at large whether good or bad because of the four to five years time period given to the governing party by the so-called election mandate. There are various instances in democratic style of government wherein lot of programs/ projects started by one party in power are terminated by the other party's government; for the benefit of whom; at the cost to tax payer and public's wastage of resources. You can give it any name that is it could be a policy or revenge, in both cases the hammer falls on the public heads. Normally, the governing party directs the resources for their success in future elections. Generally, the party governments being switched over election after election; leads to inconsistent domestic and foreign policies of the country where one party wants to accommodate their favorites while in government by relieving the other party's favorites from the government,

When the financial supporters of the political parties are on both sides i.e. with party in power and party in opposition in bi party countries maintaining effective control and influence over both the parties they can drive benefits from both sides of the coin. Generally, projects of longer than election terms are not taken up by the party in power as the success is attributed to the one completing the project and not, to the one who started the project. Thus, the financial supporters in a bi-party country i.e., the governing party and the opposition do influence both these parties to start projects of longer than election term or the projects that are continuously providing benefits to the financial supporters who are playing on both sides of the playing field scoring goals for both the opposing parties. This is by far not an exhaustive list of anomalies of democratic system but few of the major one's described here to elucidate the point.

CHAPTER TEN

CONCLUSION

The basic foundation of democracy is the vote and in order to get elected you have to get majority of the votes cast in your constituency. THUS THE ELIGIBLE VOTER DICTATES THE CANDIDATE AND THE POLITICAL PARTY'S CONDUCT. The various political parties in a country except single party countries DIVIDE THE NATION ON MULTI FACETS BASIS TO GET MAXIMUM VOTES FOR THEIR CANDIDATES IN ORDER TO GET ELECTED. The political party reaches the eligible voters of their nation through their leader, the candidate and the leader both as a candidate approach their local area of concern to get majority of votes in order to be elected. Thus the divided nation remains strongly divided by following the political parties, agenda and policies in a democratic style of government.

The political parties in order to get the votes of organized groups nation-wide promises the voters to vote for their candidates and if successful the PARTY WILL ACCOMMODATE THE GROUP WITH A LEGISLATION OF THEIR CHOICE, BE IT MORAL OR IMMORAL, GOOD OR BAD AND SO ON for the nation as a whole like gay groups, hunting groups, religious groups and so on.

In a country practicing democracy, ONLY THE RICH CAN AFFORD TO STAND AS CANDIDATES IN AN ELECTION BECAUSE OF THE HUGE NATURE OF EXPENCES involved and once the candidate gets elected it is his/her utmost most effort, to more than RECOVER THE MONEY SPENT in the election by affording maximum benefits (contracts, projects, etc.) to his/her business, his/her relatives, his/her close associates and friends who financed his/her campaigns and political party. Thus, the REPRESENTATIVE OF VOTERS CHANGES HANDS TO ACCOMMODATE THE PEOPLE WHO HELPED & FINANCED the campaign leaving the voters, who elected him/her, in the back seat. Thus democracy is in fact not democracy but a misnomer of plutocracy where only the plutocrats can take part as candidates.

In democracy it is very rare for the successful party to win a landslide or even get more than 50% of total eligible votes to establish itself as a party with policies/agenda for the majority of voters in a democratic country. THUS, THE PUBLIC OF A COUNTRY IS MISREPRESENTED WHERE THE POLICIES AND CHOICES OF THE GOVERNMENT ARE NOT FOR MAJORITY OF THE POPULATION. In most of the countries practicing democratic form of government, majority of the population is misrepresented by the political party legislature members forming a government.

In addition to the above direct misrepresentation of the country's population, democratic governments of most countries MISREPRESENT THE VOTERS OF THEIR OWN COUNTRY WHO CAST THEIR VOTES, ON THE BEHEST OF THE INDIRECT PARTIES where succor becomes subjugation like the ECB, World Bank, IMF and so on. Succor provides temporary relief during recessionary and stagnant times followed by the layer upon layer of heavy debt burden put on the nation by providing more funds to save it from default which then starts facing the phenomena of constantly meddling in their day to day affaires by these indirect parties for the release of every other debt installment in running the government leading to imposition of higher taxes, cuts in public spending, closing down or trimming the public organizations and services and so on, which was not, the governing party's policy/agenda in an election. Thus, the population becomes debt ridden where THE NEWLY BORN ONE'S ARE GIVEN THE GIFT OF DEBT UPON their birth which they have to pay once they join the workforce and forego all the facilities and opportunities available to them without the country being in debt; for which their ancestors have paid dearly during their times. Thus, the VOTERS OF THE FUTURE GENERATION PAY FOR THE PAST ACTIONS, OF A MISREPRESENTED DEMOCRATIC FORM OF GOVERNMENT, hijacked by different indirect parties for their own benefit who have led the population of the country into burgeoning debt, and then bully the elected democratic governments into paying the installments through non democratic cut in public spending, services and removing the subsidies.

The political party leadership office bearers elected in a democratic set up by party members to represent the party in an election REPRESENT THE PARTY MEMBERS before election who have elected them and after taking part in an election the party leadership and elected candidates represent the voters that have cast their votes for them. The elected representatives DO NOT REPRESENT THE POPULATION OF THE COUNTRY BUT ONLY THE PERCENTAGE OF ELIGIBLE AND REGISTERED VOTERS WHO HAVE VOTED THEM in the avowed representation.

To say not the last but the least the democratic form of government do not represent even the voters who voted for them when this government starts representing second, third and fourth place indirect parties like interest groups, world powers, ECB/World Bank/ IMF and so on; to get benefits for themselves like financial benefits and political benefits against affording benefits to the public of the country. The various interest groups contribute funds to gain benefits for themselves, at the expense of the public, to finance the political party and its candidates because most of these political contributions are tax deductible thereby shifting the tax burden to the public kitty by the amount shifted to the political parties and their candidates. Thus, election after election these indirect parties get powerful and rich by getting the public projects, various contracts; financial aids and grants from their government for their own benefit portraying it to be for the benefit of the country's public, whereas, the public looses the same money from public kitty which is ultimately recovered from the same public through taxes. Then there are wars fought for the benefit of a third country, at the expense of loss of life and resources of your country and target country. Then there are wars initiated against target countries, (which do not accept the third party proposals for carrying on their business agenda) at the behest of third party causing great loss of life and resources for the war initiating country in affording benefits to the third party like the sale of arms and ammunition, control of resources and so on. Thus these third parties get rich and richer by the destruction of resources and loss of life of both the the host country and the target countries , where the host and the target countries both fight somebody else's war at the expense of their own public's loss of life and resources.

The countries practicing democracy are continuously under heavy financial burden due to the funds needed for maintaining electoral rolls, electoral offices and staff, maintaining federal legislature at top with all the salaries, perks and pensions, maintaining provincial/state legislature, maintaining municipal legislatures, thus supporting layer upon layer of law making and breaking machines at a very heavy cost to the public as the same billions could be spent on the welfare of the general deserving public, and also for carrying out infrastructure projects, benevolent projects and so on for the welfare of the general public at large instead of making the richer get rich and the poor becomes poorer.

Peter Mair states, "it is often real or potential access to public office which has enhanced the ability of the parties to accommodate organizational resources such as staff and money. In this sense, the state, which is often the source of these resources, becomes a means by which parties can help ensure their own persistence and survival." (P-7) "how the state, as opposed to simple civil society, has become unquestionably important for the survival of political parties, both in terms of legitimacy which public office confers, as well as in terms of the resources and capacities which are either offered, or regulated, by state itself." (How parties organize: from civil society to the state. 1994)

Democracy in bi-party and multi party system go hand in hand with capitalism according to professor Halm in his book Comparative Economic System, "We must be particularly careful when capitalism's deficiencies are to be corrected at the price of the freedoms which are the most characteristics feature of the market economy. We, ought not to, forget that capitalism has proved its compatibility with political democracy, whereas all centrally planned systems, so far, have been totalitarian, will it be possible to maintain economic and political freedom when we aim for goals which capitalism admittedly cannot reach?"

Democracy has complemented the failing capitalism by lending huge financial support from the public kitty in the USA and Europe (IN THE NAME OF EMPLOYMENT/UNEMPLOYMNT) to their failed business friends who should have been weeded out by their business failure (where the existent law doesn't guarantee any financial support to failed businesses)

"Some seven men form an Association (if possible, all peers and Baronets). They start off with a public declaration to what extent they mean to pay their debts that's called their capital" (P.77-3500).

W.S. Gilbert

Not to mention the unequal distribution of wealth and income where there is no tax on the idle accumulated wealth, the insatiable profit motive which has lead to the movement of capital to low manufacturing cost countries with ever diminishing industrial base of high cost manufacturing countries, thus eroding the foundations of service and banking sectors which remain constantly over-expanded in the face of diminishing industrial sector, where the competitive struggle in the light of modern technologies is leading to monopolistic tendencies with decreasing level of employment resulting in prolonged and expanding mass unemployment under burgeoning debt burden eating the tax payers money (where the right to tax someone gives the tax payer the right to claim benefits of its disbursement.) Thus the right of the tax payer to claim benefits of disbursement is being surrendered in favor of organizations and countries that have extended the funds to create the debt in their country.

"DEMOCRACY GIVES EVERY MAN THE RIGHT TO BE HIS OWN OPPRESSOR "JAMES RUSTER LOWER.(70-3500)

As against the above, one person rule; who considers himself/ herself as servant of the people and is God fearing as well as can treat the whole population as equal subjects and is not a ruler, tyrant, or a dictator, would lead to way far lower taxes by eliminating the huge democratic form of government expenses, consistent long term policies(as the government do not change hands every four to five years) on the domestic and international fronts, swiftness in making changes for the benefit of the population of a country, and to say not the last but the least it is easier to convince one than to fight with many. A happy unified nation; not governed by the rich (Plutocrats) whose conduct is dictated by the voters, who will vote them in; there are no conservatives, no liberals, no democrats, no republicans, no left, no right; the whole population is represented as equal subjects and not just a small percentage of voters, laws made for all the subjects and not for the voting groups. Alas! What will the communication channels do to keep them busy and flourishing?

BIBLIOGRAPHY
BOOKS

1.   CHARLES W. KEGELEY JR. – EUGENE R. WITIKOPF "WORLD POLITICS – TREND AND TRANSFORMATION – 2004 WADSWORTH.

2.   GERALD F. LIEBERMAN, "3500 GOOD QUOTES FOR SPEAKERS" PUBLISHED BY DOUBLEDAY 1983.

3.   HALM, "COMPARATIVE ECONOMIC SYSTEMS," 1963.

4.   HERBERT E. ALEXANDER AND MONICA BAUER – "FINANCEING THE 1988 ELECTIONS," – WESTVIEW PRESS 1991.

5.   JOHN DUN"POLITICAL OBLIGATIONS IN ITS HISTORICAL CONTEXT,"CAMBRIDGE UNIVERSITY PRESS 1980.

6.   KENNETHJANDA"POLITICALPARTIES.ACROSS NATIONAL SURVEY," 1980.

7.   LORD ACTON LLD (PLANNED BY) EDITED BY A.W.WARD LITT.D-G.W.PROTHERO LITT.D, STANELY LEATHES M.A."THE CAMBRIDGE MODERN HISTORY – 1902-1969- REPRINTED BY CAMBRIDGE UNIVERSITY PRESS.

8.   MICHAELGALLAGHERAND PAUL MITCHELL – "THE POLITICS OF ELECTORAL SYSTEMS." OXFOD UNIVERSITY PRESS – 2005-2006.

9.   MONTE PALMER AND WILLIAM R. THOMPSON – "THE COMPARATIVE ANALYSIS OF POLITICS" F.E. PEACOCK PUBLISHERS 1978.

10.   RICHARD S. KATZ AND PETER MAIR (EDITORS), "HOW PARTIES ORGANIZE – CHANGE AND ADAPTATION IN PARTY ORGANIZATIONS IN WESTERN DEMOCRACIES, "SAGE PUBLICATIONS – 1994.

11.   SIR, IVOR JENNINGS, "THE STUFF OF POLITICS CAMBRIDGE," 1962 VOLUME III.

12.   VERNON   BOGDANOR   AND   DAVID   BUTLER, "DEMOCRACY AND ELECTIONS – ELECTORAL SYSTEMS AND THEIR POLITICAL CONSEQUENCIES," CAMBRIDGE UNIVERSITY PRESS – 1982.

13.   W.W.ROSTOW,"POLITICS   AND   THE   STAGES   OF GROWTH," CAMBRIDGE UNIVERSITY PRESS – 1971.

NEWSPAPERS:

"THE DAWN"

FRIDAY MARCH 5, 2010; FRIDAY MAY 14,2010; MONDAY MAY17, 2010; FRIDAY MAY 21, 2010; WEDNESDAY JUNE 8, 2011; FRIDAY JUNE 24, 2011; FRIDAY SEPTEMBER 30, 2011; SATURDAY OCTOBER 01, 2011; FRIDAY OCTOBER 07, 2011; TUESDAY OCTOBER 25,2011; WEDNESDAY OCTOBER 05, 2011;

"THE NEWS"

SATURDAY MARCH 05, 2011. THURSDAY JUNE 30, 2011. SUNDAY OCTOBER 09, 2011. SATURDAY APRIL30, 2011

"DAILY TIMES"

SUNDAY OCTOBER 23, 2011.

"THE NATION"

SUNDAY OCTOBER 02, 2011.